CAIRO

By Malise Ruthven
and the Editors of Time-Life Books

Photographs by Robert Azzi

THE GREAT CITIES · TIME-LIFE BOOKS · AMSTERDAM

The Author: Malise Ruthven was born in Dublin in 1942. After graduating from Cambridge University, he studied Arabic in Lebanon before becoming a writer and editor for the BBC Arabic Service. In 1974 he turned to freelance work as a writer and commentator on Middle East affairs. His book, *Torture: The Grand Conspiracy,* an historical study of torture from classical to modern times, was published in 1978.

The Photographer: Born in 1943 in New Hampshire, Robert Azzi is a prize-winning American photojournalist who has covered major political issues in the Middle East since 1969. His work has appeared in the *National Geographic* and FORTUNE magazines, and in 1976 he studied at Harvard University as a Nieman Fellow in Journalism. His comprehensive photographic study, *An Arabian Portfolio,* was awarded a Kodak Fotobuchpreis in Germany in 1977, and a second book, *A Saudi-Arabian Portfolio,* was published in 1979.

TIME-LIFE INTERNATIONAL
EUROPEAN EDITOR: Kit van Tulleken
Design Director: Louis Klein
Photography Director: Pamela Marke
Chief of Research: Vanessa Kramer
Special Projects Editor: Windsor Chorlton
Chief Sub-Editor: Ilse Gray

THE GREAT CITIES
Series Editor: Deborah Thompson
Editorial Staff for *Cairo*
Text Editor: Alan Dingle
Designer: Joyce Mason
Picture Editor: Christine Hinze
Staff Writers: Mike Brown, Anthony Masters
Text Researcher: Jackie Matthews
Sub-Editor: Nicoletta Flessati
Design Assistants: Susan Altman, Adrian Saunders
Editorial Assistants: Kathryn Coutu, Stephanie Lindsay
Proof-Reader: Brian Sambrook

Editorial Production:
Production Editor: Ellen Brush
Traffic Co-ordinators: Pat Boag, Helen Whitehorn
Picture Department: Sarah Dawson, Belinda Stewart Cox
Art Department: Julia West
Editorial Department: Ajaib Singh Gill

The captions and the texts accompanying the photographs in this volume were prepared by the editors of TIME-LIFE Books.

Published by TIME-LIFE International (Nederland) B.V.
Ottho Heldringstraat 5, Amsterdam 1018.

© 1980 TIME-LIFE International (Nederland) B.V.
All rights reserved. First printing in English.

No part of this book may be reproduced in any form or by any electronic or mechanical means, including information storage and retrieval devices or systems, without prior written permission from the publisher, except that brief passages may be quoted for review.

ISBN 7054 0505 2

Cover: The blocks of polished limestone encasing the summit of the Pyramid of Khafre are all that remain of the facing that once fully sheathed the structure's solid core of coarser limestone: most of the façade was removed in medieval times to provide building materials for Cairo monuments. Khafre's Pyramid, second largest of the famous group of pharaonic tombs at Gizah on the south-west fringe of the capital, was completed some 4,500 years ago.

First end paper: Hieroglyphic texts, almost perfectly preserved, completely cover a chamber wall inside a pyramid at Saqqarah —some 20 miles south of Cairo. The tomb was built for the 5th-Dynasty Pharaoh Unas ; the inscriptions are religious formulae meant to aid the dead king on his journey into the afterlife.

Last end paper: Unglazed flowerpots are attractively stacked for sale along a roadside on the southern fringe of Cairo, where the city's open-air potteries are located. The pots are made of silt and clay from the Nile, by techniques that have been handed down for more than 5,000 years.

TIME LIFE BOOKS

THE SEAFARERS
WORLD WAR II
THE GOOD COOK
THE TIME-LIFE ENCYCLOPAEDIA OF GARDENING
HUMAN BEHAVIOUR
THE GREAT CITIES
THE ART OF SEWING
THE OLD WEST
THE WORLD'S WILD PLACES
THE EMERGENCE OF MAN
LIFE LIBRARY OF PHOTOGRAPHY
THIS FABULOUS CENTURY
TIME-LIFE LIBRARY OF ART
FOODS OF THE WORLD
GREAT AGES OF MAN
LIFE SCIENCE LIBRARY
LIFE NATURE LIBRARY
YOUNG READERS LIBRARY
LIFE WORLD LIBRARY
THE TIME-LIFE BOOK OF BOATING
TECHNIQUES OF PHOTOGRAPHY
LIFE AT WAR
LIFE GOES TO THE MOVIES
BEST OF LIFE

Contents

I

"The Big City"

I cannot remember a time when I was unaware of Cairo. Throughout my childhood in the quiet southern English town of Windsor, I often heard my mother and grandparents speak in nostalgic tones about Egypt's capital—as they did also about Baghdad, Tripoli, Palestine and other exotic-sounding places in the Middle East. The fortunes of my family had long been bound up with Egypt, the Nile and the desert.

From Cairo my grandfather, a young militia officer, had in 1898 set out southwards for the Sudan, to join General Kitchener's British and Egyptian troops in their struggle to restore Anglo-Egyptian rule after a nationalist uprising. He had won the Victoria Cross, Britain's highest military decoration, for his daring rescue of an Egyptian officer—an action that laid the foundation for a spectacular army career. My father, also a soldier, was sent to fight in the North Africa campaign early in the Second World War. In order to be near him, my mother contrived to get herself a job in Cairo, making propaganda for the Allies amongst the sometimes sceptical Egyptians. There, in a city overshadowed by the threat of invasion, my parents enjoyed an all-too-brief interlude of happiness; and there I was conceived. In late 1941 my mother sailed for home, running the gauntlet of German U-boats so that I could be born in a Dublin nursing home. My father had meanwhile joined a commando group and, after the Allied victory at El Alamein in the autumn of 1942, he led raids on the retreating German and Italian forces. He was wounded and captured; and on Christmas Eve, 1942, died of his injuries in an Italian military hospital.

The city through which my forebears passed on their way to meet such differing destinies had captivated the minds of men for centuries before it became a focus of my own childhood vision. In my imagination, fed by stories from the *Arabian Nights*, I pictured Cairo as a fabulous place of stately domes and minarets, mysterious bazaars and warm, scented evenings; a city peopled by mustachioed warriors in turbans, crafty servants and enigmatic, veiled women in long, flowing robes—much like the robe my mother sometimes wore when dressing for dinner. When I finally came to visit Cairo, I found that my boyhood dreams—though inevitably erased by reality—were richly replaced.

The city sprawls along the banks of the Nile in northern Egypt, just south of the point where the river divides to form its broad, fertile delta. This strategic location, astride both the Nile and the overland caravan trails from Arabia and Palestine to North Africa—the arteries along which Egypt's agricultural and commercial wealth has flowed from time immem-

From its pedestal on the island of Gezirah, a statue of Sa'ad Zaghlul, Egypt's great nationalist leader of the 1920s, overlooks two fishing boats drifting on a stretch of the Nile that runs through the heart of Cairo. Beyond, on the river's west bank, looms a high-rise hotel, typical of the skyscrapers that proliferated throughout the city in the 1960s and 1970s.

orial—has been the site of a thriving community since the 6th Century B.C. and the seat of the nation's rulers since the 7th Century A.D. But Egypt has paid a price for her prosperity; for two and a half millennia, between 525 B.C. and 1952, every one of her rulers was of foreign blood—leaders of the Persians, Greeks, Romans, Arabs, Turks and British who were lured there by the country's seemingly inexhaustible fecundity.

In the Middle Ages, at least, the covetousness of the conquerors was understandable, for Cairo was one of the richest and most populous cities in the world; her glories were extravagantly praised by poets and travellers alike. Consider this panegyric, written some 600 years ago:

He who hath not seen Cairo hath not seen the world.
Her soil is gold,
Her Nile is a marvel,
Her women are the bright-eyed houris of Paradise,
Her houses are palaces, and her air is soft, with an odour above
    aloes, refreshing the heart;
And how should Cairo be otherwise, when she is the Mother of
    the World?

A century later, a traveller who was familiar with the great trading towns of Europe was inspired to write: "If it were possible to place . . . Rome, Milan, Padua and Florence together with four other cities, they would not . . . contain the wealth and population of the half of Cairo."

Today's fellahin, the rural peasants who are the native stock of much-conquered Egypt, still proudly refer to their capital as *Misr, Umm al-Dunyah*—"Cairo, Mother of the World". *Misr* is an ancient Semitic word that has been current since the earliest recorded time, meaning simply "big city". But Cairo has for so long dominated the thoughts of Egyptians that its inhabitants have come to use Misr impartially to describe both their country and its capital.

Thus it was with great expectations that, in 1969, I paid my first visit. Having arrived by sea at Alexandria, Egypt's chief port and second city, I boarded the train for the 135-mile journey south-east to the capital. For the best part of three hours we rolled slowly across the Nile delta, a flat, unchanging landscape of rich, green, intensively cultivated fields, punctuated at intervals by untidy villages of single-storey mud-brick houses. As the train penetrated the outer suburbs of Cairo, the fields vanished and a scruffy, urban dilapidation crowded in. There were innumerable streets of tiny dwellings, much like the ones in the country-side, and on the flat roofs animal fodder was laid out to dry, looking like tufts of unbrushed hair. Goats, donkeys and brown-skinned infants competed for space in narrow thoroughfares festooned with washing; other children splashed about happily amongst water-buffaloes in the foetid canals that ran parallel with the railway tracks. Just as I was beginning to think that this enormous village would go on forever, the

Traffic, including heavily loaded donkey carts and crowds of pedestrians, mingles in colourful confusion on the Shari' al-Qal'ah, one of the broad, European-style streets that were cut through the city's medieval quarters in the late 19th Century. Abetted by the numerous draught animals that impede the pace of motor vehicles, Cairo's citizens habitually walk in the roadway.

train shuddered to a halt at Cairo Station, the main-line terminal, situated at the northern edge of the city centre.

Getting out of the air-conditioned carriage was like opening the door of a blast-furnace; although the people of Cairo take pride in their city's pleasant winter climate, it was early summer when I arrived. Fighting for breath in the afternoon heat, I struggled out of the crowded station and found myself a taxi to take me to my intended hotel, the Nile Hilton. The driver roared off into the thick of a fuming phalanx of traffic that ground its way slowly down a boulevard lined with European-style buildings six or eight storeys high. We jockeyed aggressively for position among trucks belching clouds of poisonous black smoke and battered buses jammed to overflowing with sweltering humanity. Passengers who could not find room inside the buses clung outside to window-frames, door handles and even the bodies of other hangers-on.

People were everywhere, thronging the pavements, pouring in and out of shops and offices, leaning out of windows, or strolling casually into the path of oncoming vehicles. There were dark-eyed peasant girls, colourful in print dresses and headscarves; graceful Nubian youths wearing turbans and dazzling white cotton *galabiyahs*, the traditional loose-fitting Egyptian garment that resembles a nightgown; plump, bourgeois matrons in tight blouses and precarious stiletto heels; sallow-faced, mustachioed civil servants; and middle-aged businessmen wearing the short-sleeved hybrid pyjama-cum-safari suit particularly popular among Egyptians. Animals—indispensable as both food and transport in Cairo—were almost as numerous as people; sheep nuzzled at scraps of nameless rubbish on the pavement, and donkeys with eyes modestly downcast strained as they pulled at carts piled with scrap-metal. I saw a camel reclining in the back of a truck, lazily chewing its cud and batting its eyelashes at the passers-by.

Everyone seemed to consider it a duty to make as much noise as possible: drivers leant on their horns for minutes on end or coaxed ear-splitting roars from their unmuffled engines, and the plaintive sound of Arab music seeped from a thousand radios. Over the scene hung an acrid haze compounded of petrol fumes, sand blown in from the desert and the greasy smoke from mutton kebabs being cooked at kerbside stalls.

After what seemed like hours of snail-like progress, my driver, who had never ceased to ply me with friendly questions about where I was from and what I was going to do in Cairo, turned off the main thoroughfare into a *maydan*—a square—and, elated by his new-found freedom, accelerated straight towards a crowd of schoolchildren. I shut my eyes, clung to the seat and waited for the squeal of brakes and the thud of a small body against the radiator. Miraculously, the throng of children parted before the speeding taxi and closed again behind it, like clouds around an aircraft.

At last I was deposited safely at the Hilton, an anonymous modern block, faced with multicoloured mosaics, that stands by the Nile's edge,

A burst of fireworks illuminates the night sky above the 590-foot-high Cairo Tower during celebrations to mark the prophet Muhammad's birthday in the third month of the Muslim calendar. The edifice, built on the island of Gezirah in 1957, is surmounted by a revolving restaurant and a radio and television mast.

south-west of the city centre. Within half an hour I was seated comfortably at the window of my hotel room, contemplating a hundred feet below the broad, grey-green river flowing lazily past, and attempting to collect my thoughts. Could this frenetic, crowded, disorderly city really be the Cairo that my family and their friends had spoken of as the most exotic capital in the world, livelier than Paris or Vienna, more cosmopolitan than Rome or New York? I simply could not believe it. Obviously, my chaotic first impressions, gained in the battleground of the streets, were not to be relied upon; what I needed was a vantage point from which I could take a more detached view of the city.

An ideal viewpoint at once presented itself to me as I looked across the river. Flowing northwards through the centre of the city, the Nile encircles in succession two large and populous islands, both of them shaped like elongated leaves. Directly opposite me was the southern extremity of Gezirah (the Arabic word meaning "island"), about two-and-a-half miles long; a hundred yards upstream to my left lay the slightly smaller island of Rawdah. From the elegant parkland that occupies half of Gezirah rises the 590-foot Cairo Tower, a hollow cylinder enclosed by concrete lattice walls rising to a decorative top that is modelled, not entirely successfully, on the lotus-bud motif of ancient Egyptian art. The tower was built in 1957; surmounting it is a restaurant that revolves slowly, providing diners with a non-stop panorama of Cairo. Or rather, it is supposed to; whether because of defective bearings or insufficient power, it is usually immobile. The more cynical inhabitants of Cairo liken its progress to that of the Egyptian Revolution of 1952: it took one turn, then stopped.

The morning after my arrival, I strolled out of the hotel, crossed Tahrir (Liberation) Bridge to Gezirah and rode the lift to the top of the tower; there may be other, more romantic ways to view Cairo, but none of them offers such a comprehensive vista. Under a scorching haze of sand and dust—the ever-present reminder of the surrounding desert—Cairo sprawls for miles in every direction, a tightly woven tapestry of pale-grey and dark-brown buildings, hemmed in to the east by the tawny limestone cliffs of the Muqattam Hills and fading away to the west into the great expanse of the North African desert.

My eye was immediately drawn to the Nile at the foot of the tower. The river bisects the city from south to north like a huge gleaming scimitar, at least half a mile wide at its broadest point, flowing with the unrippled smoothness of a mighty body of water. Since all but one twentieth of Egypt's land is arid, unproductive desert, this single waterway is her supreme natural resource. Indeed, for thousands of years Egyptians depended for their very survival on the Nile's annual flood in late summer. These inundations, caused by spring rains some 1,500 miles south in the mountains of Ethiopia, regularly spread a thick layer of rich, black mud

Seen from the Cairo Tower, the Nile flows northwards on the last stage of its journey from the heart of Africa, passing beneath the bridges that connect Rawdah

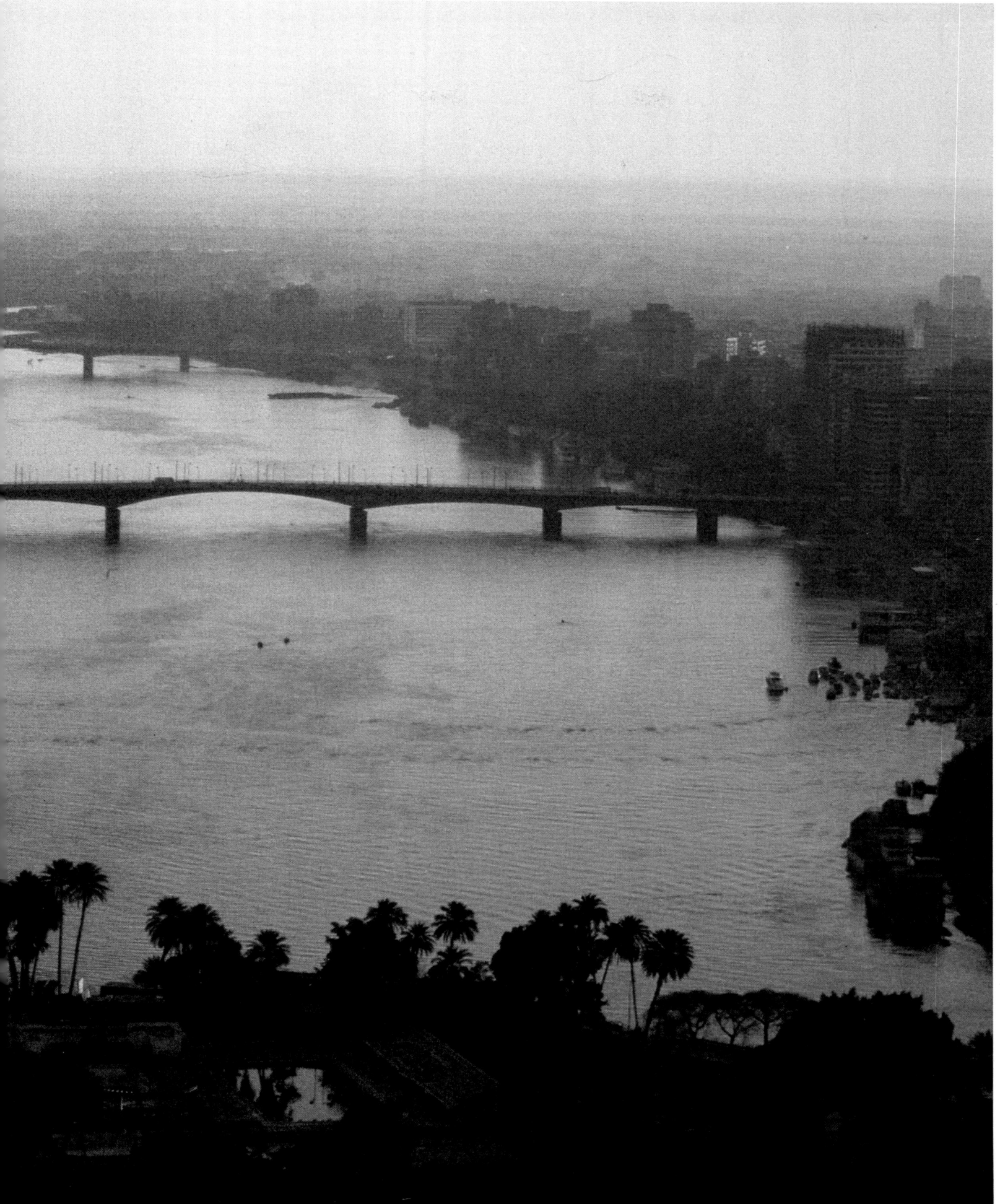

land (left) with Cairo's west bank. After a rare shower has cleared the dusty air, the 4,700-year-old pyramids at Saqqarah are dimly visible 20 miles to the south.

over the riverside fields, renewing their fertility and keeping the hungry desert at bay. But the Nile could be capricious: sometimes the flood failed, bringing famine to Egypt, and sometimes it came with excessive fury, sweeping away crops, livestock and even entire villages. Since 1970, however, with the completion of the Aswan High Dam 600 miles upstream from Cairo, the river has been finally tamed and floods no more.

The Nile has dictated the pattern of human settlement in Egypt. Measuring 4,160 miles, it is the longest river in the world, rising as the White Nile from Uganda's Lake Victoria, deep in the plateau of equatorial Africa; three quarters of its immense journey is already over by the time it crosses Egypt's southern frontier at Lake Nasser, the inland sea that has built up behind the Aswan High Dam. The river then begins a leisurely passage through the valley of Upper—that is, southern—Egypt, a thickly populated strip of well-watered farmland, fringed with serrated cliffs that were cut by the Nile as it forged its ancient course to the Mediterranean. On either side of this green ribbon, which is seldom more than 12 miles wide, stretches the desert.

Cairo stands at the northern extremity of Upper Egypt. Twelve miles after the Nile has flowed through the capital, it splits into two great branches, the Rosetta and the Damietta, for the last lap of its progress towards the Mediterranean. The 10,000 square miles of land lying between these two branches was once an estuary that silted up millennia ago to form the Delta, also known as Lower Egypt; its fertile, alluvial soil, criss-crossed with irrigation canals, produces each year a crop of cotton and two or three crops of maize, rice and clover; it supports 60 per cent of Egypt's rural population. There is still truth in the remark made more than 2,400 years ago by the Greek historian Herodotus, that: "Egypt is the gift of the Nile."

Viewed from my vantage point on the Cairo Tower, the great life-giving flow seemed calm and unhurried, more like a lake than a river. On its broad surface a streamlined pleasure-cruiser was passing with tourists leaning over the deck-rail, and I saw one or two graceful feluccas, the traditional Egyptian river boat, with a triangular sail reminiscent of a swallow's wing, that has not changed in shape since the day when Cleopatra made her historic progress down the Nile with Mark Antony. The grand riverside boulevards—the Corniche of the east bank and the Shari' al-Nil on the west—were lined with stately palms, their rich foliage enlivening the city's prevailing sunburnt hue. Moored along the narrow channel of the Nile that divides Gezirah from the river's west bank, I could see a few neglected, but still elegant, houseboats with wooden verandahs and ornate shutters. In midstream, a solitary fisherman stood in the stern of his tiny row-boat and cast his net into the river.

Crowding in from all sides on these peaceful scenes was the modern city. Cairo's site is shaped like a fan, with the narrow end to the south,

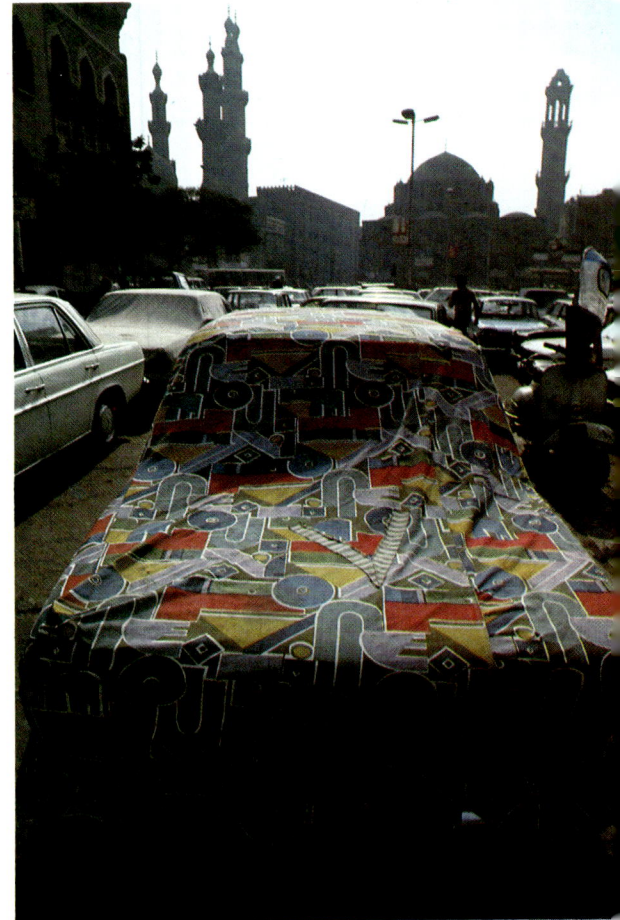

Parked outside the ancient al-Azhar mosque located in the centre of the medieval city, an automobile is protected from Cairo's pervasive dust and blistering midday sun by a multicoloured canvas envelope. Although only one in 25 Cairenes owns a private vehicle, lack of public parking space and indiscriminate street parking contribute greatly to the city's traffic problems.

where the sandstone plateaux of the desert converge on the river, and widening to the north, where the valley spreads out into the Delta. The natural barrier of the Muqattam Hills two miles to the east, and gradual changes in the river's course over the centuries have governed the stages of the city's development, so that it is laid out, roughly speaking, in three parallel bands running north and south. As I scanned the city from the tower, I could make out various distinct neighbourhoods that, even from such a remove, obviously had different characteristics.

Immediately to the east of the tower, on my right as I looked down-stream, the downtown commercial sector of Cairo spread along the Nile's east bank, the sunlight glinting on the plate-glass windows of its tall office blocks, apartment buildings and luxury hotels, and on the roofs of the traffic funnelling down its wide, straight avenues. It was a sight that could have been duplicated in any thriving metropolis in the world. But among the concrete slabs, glimpses of an older and grander style of architecture reminded me that this was an area originally laid out in the 1860s, in conscious imitation of Baron Haussmann's then recent rebuilding of Paris. Its construction was made possible by a gradual westward drift in the river's course, caused by silting, that in time created fresh expanses of usable land on the east bank.

But the city had been founded further east. Squeezed between the concrete towers of modern Cairo and the dusty escarpment of the Muqattam Hills was a patch of lower, brown buildings, with dozens of ornate minarets rising above them. This area of Cairo—a teeming warren of narrow alley-ways, mud-brick houses and ancient mosques—constitutes the Old City, the lineal descendant of the populous and fabulously rich metropolis of the Middle Ages.

Cairo has had a complicated history. The first settlement on the city's present site was three miles further south-west than the surviving Old City. Begun as a small fortress known as Babylon, it was built by the invading Persians, conquerors of the Pharaohs in 525 B.C., to guard an important crossing of the Nile.

During the ensuing centuries, when Egypt fell to other conquerors (the Greeks, led by that youthful prodigy Alexander the Great, came in 332 B.C.; they were followed in 31 B.C. by the Romans), Babylon remained an insignificant garrison town; at this period Egypt's capital was Alexandria, the resplendent city founded by Alexander near the westernmost mouth of the Nile. Today, nothing remains of Babylon but a Roman fort, much rebuilt, sheltering within its walls several venerable churches belonging to the Copts, Egypt's earliest Christian community; they were converted in the 1st Century A.D. and still form an influential minority amongst Cairo's predominantly Muslim population.

But with the coming of Islam, Cairo became Egypt's capital and began her rise to world prominence. In A.D. 641 a cavalry army from Arabia,

GIZAH

Zoological Gardens

Shari' al-Nil

Gizah Bridge

Gam'ah Bridge

NILE RIVER

Nilometer

RAWDAH ISLAND

Shari' al-Rawdah

Mu'allaqah Church

● Coptic Museum

Corniche

GARDEN CITY

Shepheard's Hotel

MISR AL-QADIMAH

● 'Amr ibn al-'As Mosque

BAB AL-LUQ

al-Fustat

Salah Salem Avenue

● Sayyidatna Zaynab Mosque

SAYYIDAH ZAYNAB

'ABDIN

Shari' Port Sa'id

Aqueduct

Ibn Tulun Mosque

Shari' al-Qal'a

Sultan Hassan Mosque

SOUTHERN CEMETERY

● Imam al-Shafi'i Mausoleum

● Mamluk Tombs

Muhammad 'Ali Mosque

Citadel

BAB AL-KHALQ

Shari' Bab al-Wazir

al-Qahirah Walls

Salah Salem Avenue

EASTERN CEMETERY

Main Map Labels

IMBABAH

ZAMALIK

Shari' al-Nil

Cairo Tower

Gezirah Sporting Club

GEZIRAH ISLAND

26 July Bridge

6 October Bridge

Tahrir Bridge

Corniche

Shari' 26 July

BULAQ

Hilton

Egyptian Museum

Tahrir Square

Shari' al-Tahrir

Shari' Qasr al-Nil

Shari' Talat Harb

Ramses Street

Opera Square

Azbakiyah Gardens

AZBAKIYAH

Shari' Clot Bay

Ramses Square

Cairo Station

...in Palace

Shari' al-Azhar

Shari' Gawhar al-Qa'id

Shari' Port Sa'id

Shari' al-Gaysh

al-Qahirah Walls

MUSKI

Shari' al-Mu'izz

Zuwaylah

al-Ghawri Mosque

Qala'un Mosque

al-Hakim Mosque

Khan al-Khalili

Bab al-Futuh

Sayyidna al-Husayn Mosque

Bayt al-Sihaymi

Bab al-Nasr

OLD CITY

...l-Azhar Mosque

'ABBASIYAH

Inset Map Labels

SHUBRA AL KHAYMAH

Heliopolis

SHUBRA

NASR CITY

IMBABAH

CAIRO

4.7 Miles

Muqattam Hills

MUQATTAM CITY

GIZAH

Nile River

AL-MA'ADI

Gizah Pyramids

Saqqarah Pyramids

HALWAN

Daughter of the Nile

Flowing northwards through the heart of Cairo, the River Nile is the key to the city's pattern of growth. Cairo stands a hundred miles south of the Nile's Mediterranean outlets, at the apex of the fertile Delta. There have been cities near this strategic site since pharaonic times, when the Pyramids were built at nearby Gizah (inset map, below); but modern Cairo's direct ancestor was the Islamic city of al-Qahirah, founded in A.D. 969 on the east bank, where most of the city's historic monuments cluster together in the medieval Old City and its maze-like adjacent quarters (main map, left).

From the 19th Century onwards, improved flood control and stabilization of the river banks permitted successive bands of development, first on the east bank and the two large islands of Rawdah and Gezirah, and then on the west bank. In the 20th Century, rapid population expansion, especially since the 1950s, has caused the city to spread to the north and south along both banks of the Nile, and eastwards into the desert.

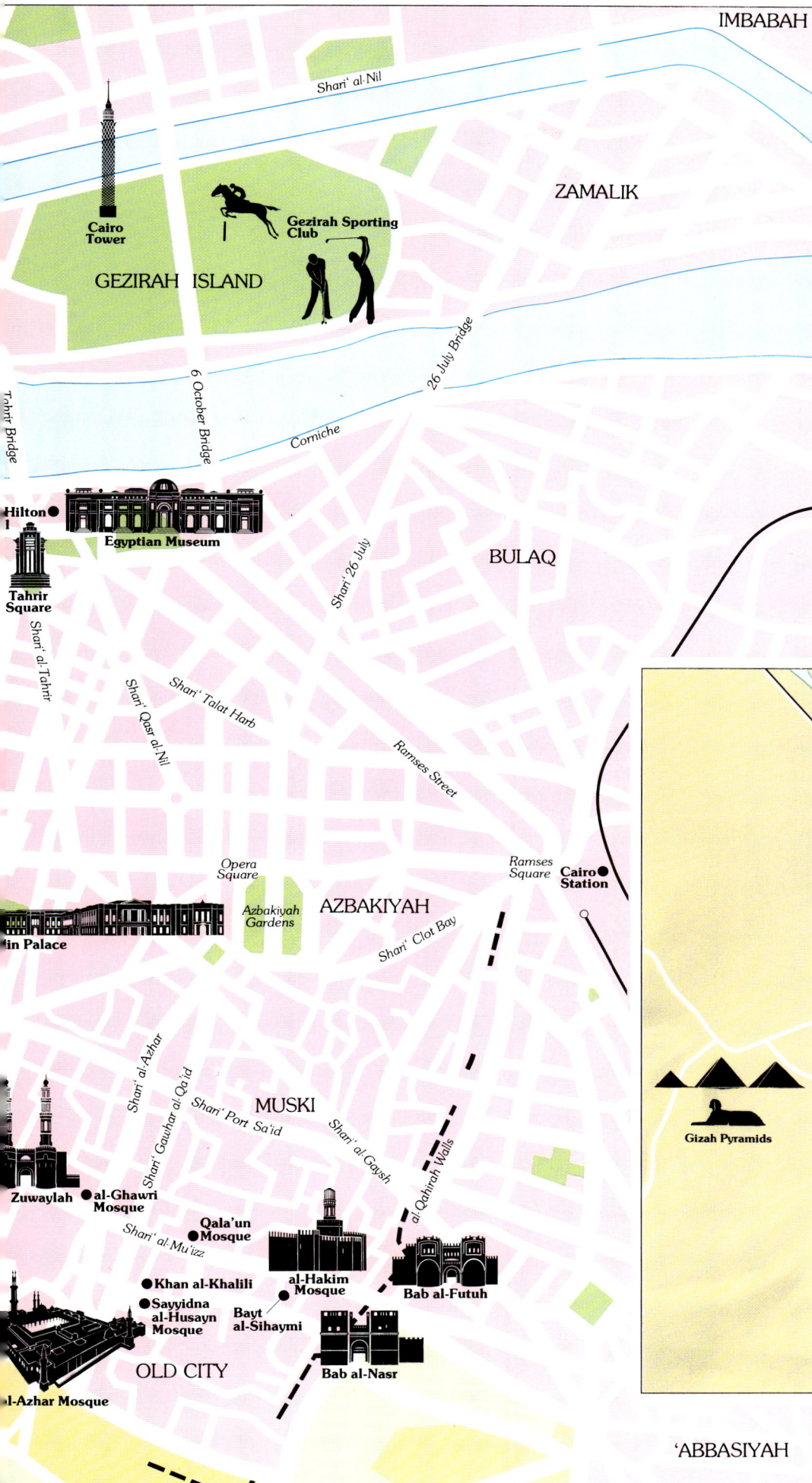

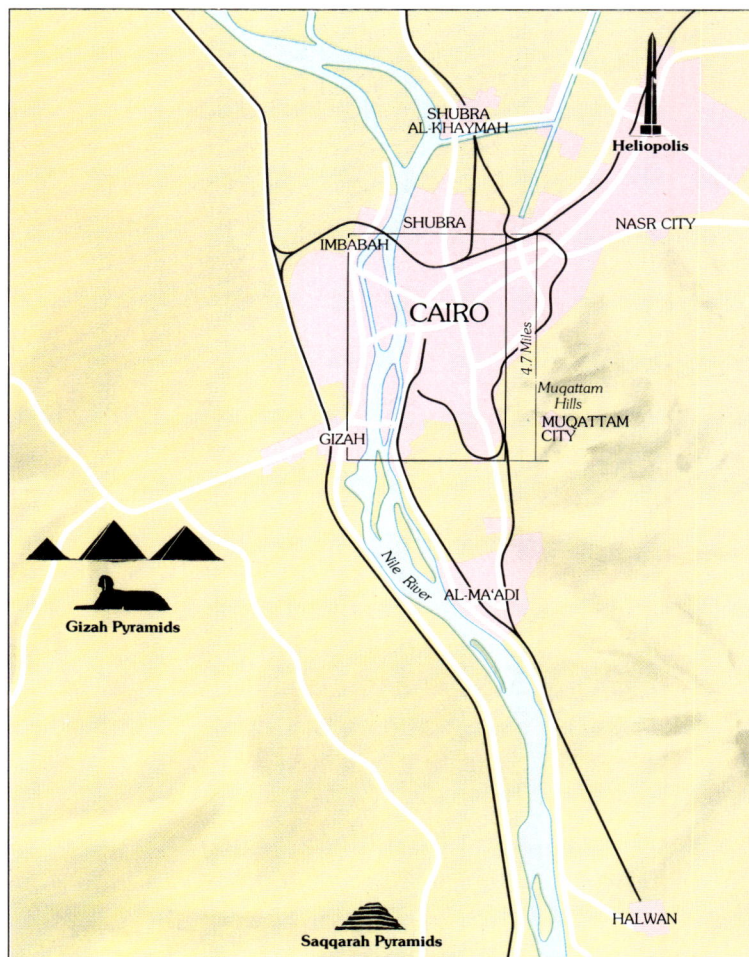

where the great expansion of the Muslim religion began, seized Egypt and set about transforming her into the Muslim country she has remained ever since. The invaders, accustomed to mobile desert warfare, were scornful of Babylon's confining walls and, according to their custom, built themselves a new settlement—known as al-Fustat, "the Encampment"— immediately to the east. This town grew into a flourishing commercial centre that superseded Alexandria; Nasir-i Khusraw, a Persian traveller who visited al-Fustat in 1047, saw 14-storey houses containing as many as 300 people, mosques crammed with thousands of worshippers and markets where dozens of different varieties of exotic flowers could be bought. Yet today, nothing remains of the city but a much-rebuilt mosque. For more than eight centuries the site was covered by a dreary wasteland of smoking rubbish heaps, until in the 1960s a government housing project was undertaken on the land of the old "Encampment"; much of the once-desolate area is now occupied by modern blocks.

In the years following the foundation of al-Fustat, power shifted within the Islamic world and two more conquerors—al-Saleh, a general acting on behalf of the 'Abbasid caliphs of Baghdad, and later Ibn Tulun, a Turk— came to Egypt. They built new cities beside al-Fustat, strung along the north-easterly curve of high ground at the foot of the Muqattam Hills, out of reach of the Nile's annual flood. These were palace-cities, reserved for the ruler, his ministers, harem and servants, and bore much the same relationship to al-Fustat as Louis XIV's Versailles did to Paris.

But all three of these early communities were destined to be over-whelmed by al-Qahirah, "the Victorious", the magnificent walled city founded in the 10th Century by yet more invaders, this time a Muslim dynasty from Tunisia. Al-Qahirah—whose name returning Italian merchants introduced to Europe in the form of "Cairo"—eventually grew into the glittering medieval metropolis that I had read about so eagerly as a child, and it is still embodied in the jumbled buildings and narrow streets of today's Old City. Al-Fustat, which expanded to swallow up the two intervening cities, co-existed with al-Qahirah for two centuries, but its fate was ignominious in the end; it gradually declined as settlement concentrated about al-Qahirah and was finally burnt down in 1168 to prevent it from falling into the hands of invading Crusaders. Al-Qahirah is now the formal name for Egypt's capital, but Misr is still the word that most Egyptians use.

The view of the Old City is dominated by a curious complex of buildings that stand watch over it from the ridge beyond. The massive Citadel was built as a stronghold by Saladin—champion of Islam against the Christian Crusaders—who ruled Egypt from Cairo in the 12th Century. Squatting incongruously on top of the Citadel, like a great fleshy eunuch, is the mosque begun in the 1820s by Muhammad 'Ali, Viceroy of the Ottoman Turks who governed Egypt—at least in name—from 1517 to the early 20th Century. Its ample domes and pencil-thin minarets proclaim its

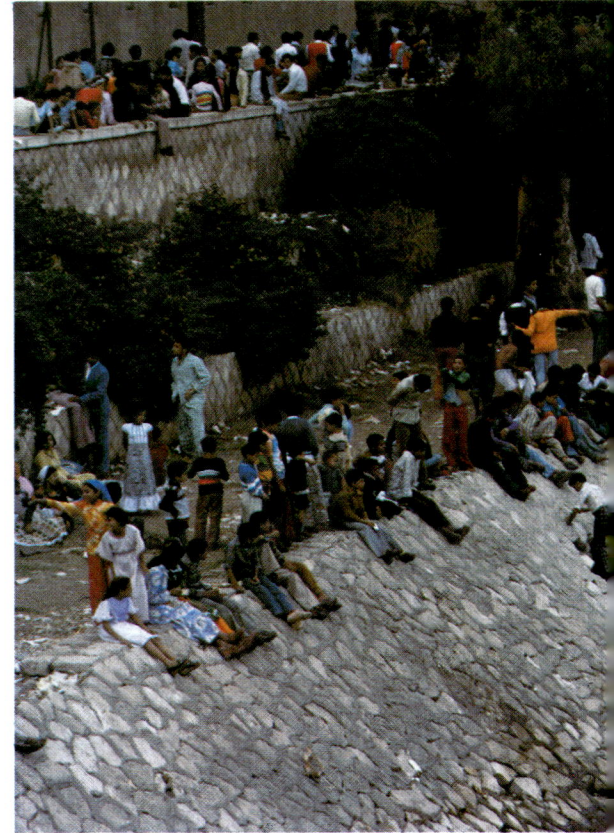

Near the southern end of Gezirah Island, young Cairenes meet to stroll and gossip on the banks of the Nile. Offering tree-shaded walks and cool, if somewhat murky, waters for swimming, the great river is one of Cairo's greatest recreational magnets.

Turkish style, quite distinct from the Cairene mosques with their sturdier minarets. On either side of the Citadel, to north and south beyond the Old City spreads the broad sweep of the city's medieval cemetery region. Known as the Cities of the Dead, these necropolises, with their spacious layouts and house-like tombs look like well-planned suburbs—and indeed thriving squatter communities have grown up among the tombs.

The band of development lying between the Old City and the east bank of the Nile was the work of Muhammad 'Ali's Ottoman dynasty in the 19th Century, but they had as their collaborators the real rulers of Egypt—the Europeans. French entrepreneurs and advisers were the first to exert their influence, from the 1820s onwards, but the British later imposed their own political and military control over Muhammad 'Ali's successors.

Most of the original 19th-Century sector has, of course, been swallowed up by modern rebuilding of the city centre, but further south along the east bank I could see the characteristically curving avenues of the Garden City, a European enclave created in the early years of the 20th Century; here and there I could make out a few survivors of the magnificent marble villas where the affluent foreigners had led their comfortable lives.

For Britons of my grandparents' and parents' generations, Cairo had appeared as a magnificent playground, even in wartime. During the 70 years of British political and military presence in Egypt, they found themselves automatically part of the ruling élite in a society that had always accorded its rulers lavish privileges. Whole quarters of the city were placed at their disposal. They swam or played tennis, golf and polo at country clubs set among lush tropical foliage and manicured lawns, lunched in the elegance of grand hotels or private clubs, and danced away the evenings in nightclubs as lively as any in London or Paris.

This privileged world, set apart from the continuing life of the city, was created by Europeans for Europeans; the British ran the government, the French and Belgians much of the industry, and the Swiss the hotels and restaurants. The foreign community behaved as if the native Egyptians existed solely to serve them, tilling the land to provide food for them, cooking for them, sweeping for them, washing their clothes, nannying their children and driving their motor cars.

Immediately below me were the green acres of a former colonial institution belonging to that world: the Gezirah Sporting Club, founded in 1882 on what had once been the palace grounds of one of the Ottoman viceroys. Its racecourse (complete with miniature grandstand), golf course, tennis courts and croquet lawns were, until the middle of this century, the exclusive preserve of British officers and their families. But the Revolution of 1952, when Egypt became an independent republic, changed everything. Today the tennis players and golfers are mostly middle-class Egyptians.

The west bank of the river, to my left, was as densely built up as the east. During the 20th Century, as improved flood control stabilized the banks,

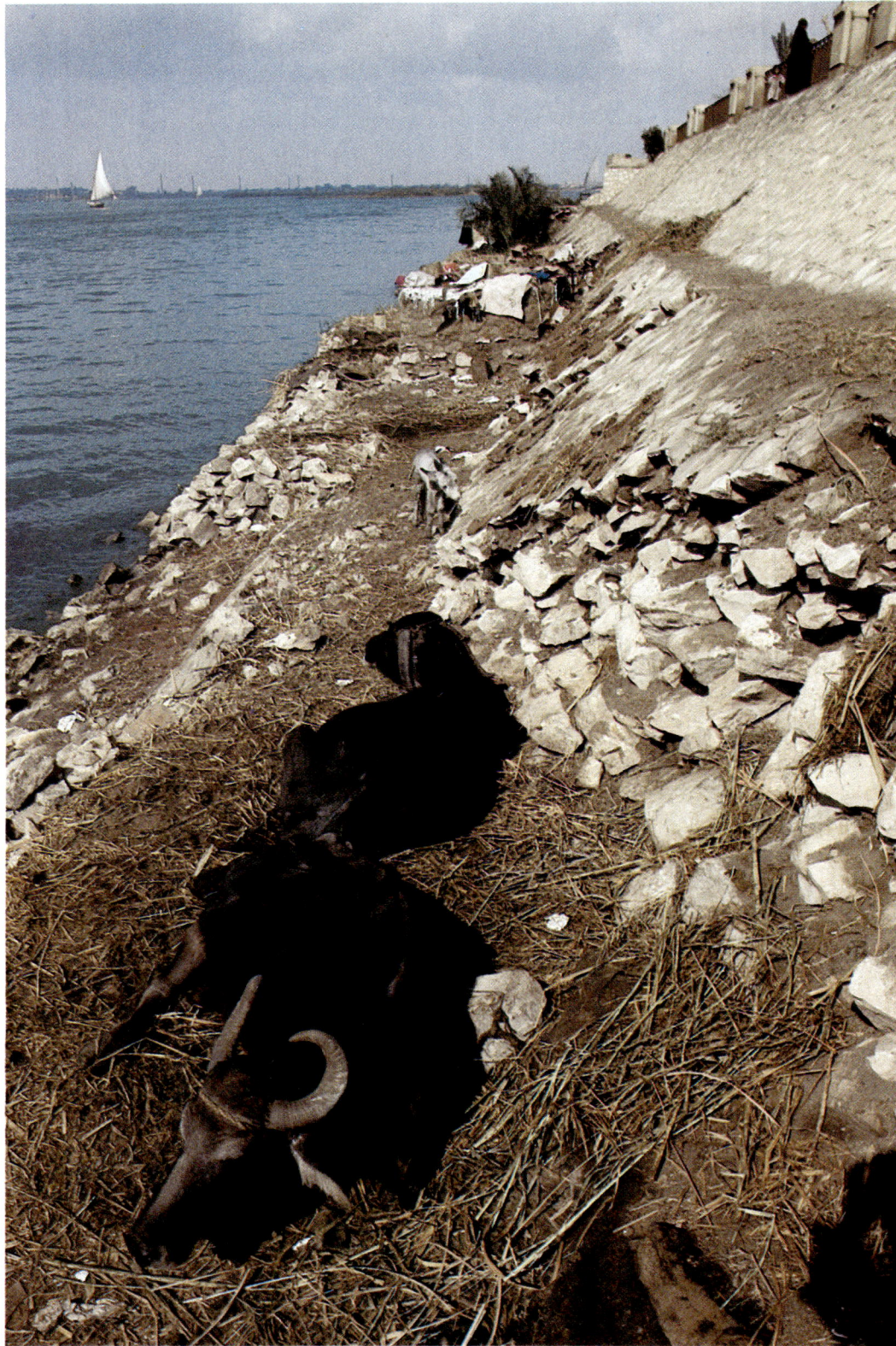

A narrow ledge on the Nile's east bank offers enough space for a family to make a home and keep livestock.

Touches of Rural Life

For some of Cairo's recent rural immigrants, the banks of the Nile afford an opportunity to continue their age-old way of life in the very heart of the modern metropolis. Freed by improved flood control from annual inundation, the narrow strips of land that lie between the water's edge and the recently built riverside boulevards offer a permanent home for numerous families, while the Nile's waters provide an unfailing resource for many more.

Against a backdrop of luxurious buildings occupying Cairo's prime riverside sites, two youths find a neglected stretch of the Nile in which to wash their sheep.

Perpetuating one of the communal habits of village life, women from a recently arrived immigrant group wash their pots together in the waters of the Nile.

the construction of several modern bridges had encouraged building on the two islands of Gezirah and Rawdah and the third band of development had begun to spread over the river's west bank.

Venerable and varied though the city of Cairo is, it is surrounded by traces of civilization more than twice as ancient. The most celebrated buildings of all that I could see from the top of the tower survive with splendour undimmed. Nine miles to the south-west, shimmering massively through the heat haze, stood the three Pyramids of Gizah. In spite of the great height of the Cairo Tower, the summits of the two larger Pyramids seemed almost on a level with my gaze. For almost 4,500 years, these enormous royal tombs have dominated the surrounding desert landscape, a source of wonder and extravagant speculation for countless generations of visitors—whether foreign invaders, tourists or scholars.

If the Pyramids are still a marvel to us, in an age when men have walked on the moon and revealed the secrets of the atom, how much more amazing they must have seemed, for instance, to the Greeks and Romans who, despite their mastery of law and military science, politics and mathematics, could never even have attempted such a combination of mass and abstract form, scale and craftsmanlike precision. It sometimes takes an effort to realize that we are now the same distance in time from Alexander the Great as he was from the builders of the Pyramids.

Twenty miles to the south, but seldom visible from Cairo through its shroud of dust, is the Step Pyramid at Saqqarah, built about 2700 B.C. and the world's oldest surviving stone structure; it stands in what was once the royal cemetery of Memphis, capital of the pharaonic kingdom from about 3100 to 2400 B.C. Little is now left of the actual city but dusty mounds and a colossal statue of the Pharaoh Ramses II.

As the largest and oldest monuments, the Pyramids seemed a logical place to begin my exploration of Cairo. I took a tram from the city centre along the Gizah road, a broad elevated carriageway built in the 1860s and nowadays lined with a variety of popular restaurants and disco-bars. When we arrived at the bare, rocky plateau on which the Pyramids stand, I was left in no doubt that I had come to Egypt's major tourist attraction. The car park was full of motor coaches, thirsty visitors queued at the soft-drinks stalls and donkey rides were offered on all sides. The more energetic tourists were clambering up the rugged sides of the Pyramids themselves.

No amount of description had prepared me for the majestic effect of those man-made mountains. One of the members of Napoleon's military expedition to Egypt in 1798 commented: "Seen from a distance they produce the same kind of effect as do high mountain peaks. . . . The nearer one approaches, the more this effect decreases. But when at last you are within a short distance of these regular masses, a wholly different impression is produced; you are struck by surprise, and as soon as you have reached the top of the slope, your ideas change in a flash. Finally, when you have reached the foot of the Great Pyramid, you are seized with a vivid and powerful emotion, tempered by a sort of stupefaction, almost overwhelming in its effects."

Sheer size is a basic element in the impression of power, mass and permanence the Pyramids create, especially when viewed from the desert side, early in the morning, or through the palm groves on the Kirdassah road in the afternoon, when the glare of the sun, filtered by the desert dust, lends them a ghostly, translucent quality. The most prominent is the 450-foot-high Great Pyramid, built about 2600 B.C. as the tomb of the Pharaoh Khufu and still the world's largest stone edifice; the area of its base is sufficient to accommodate the cathedrals of Florence, Milan and St. Peter's in Rome, together with Westminster Abbey and St. Paul's in London.

Next to it stands the fractionally smaller Pyramid of Khafre, Khufu's son, crowned by the remnants of its original polished limestone facing stones. The rest of these beautifully dressed stones have been stripped off over the centuries to be used by the builders of Cairo in their own monuments. Guarding the end of the ceremonial causeway leading from Khafre's Pyramid is the Sphinx, the huge human-headed lion whose features are thought to have been modelled on those of Khafre. The monument was carved *in situ* from a natural outcropping of sandstone. The last Pyramid in the line of three is the smaller tomb of the Pharaoh Menkaure.

These monuments represent the zenith of pharaonic power; they were laboriously constructed, in an age that was ignorant of both the wheel and the pulley, by thousands of workmen who contributed their labour as a sacred duty. The Gizah Pyramids were built to last for eternity; surveying their immense bulk looming over the ephemeral structures of later times, I felt that they stood a real chance of doing so.

The inscrutable presence of the Pyramids and the Sphinx in the desert on Cairo's outskirts has a certain paradoxical quality. They are by far the best-known features of Egypt, bringing large numbers of tourists to Cairo; yet, they have nothing at all to do with the development of the present city. Modern Egyptians are perhaps even more susceptible to the Pyramids' fascination than outsiders. In the 20th Century, pharaonic Egypt has sometimes seemed like a symbol for a concept of Egyptian national identity, counterbalancing ideas of a pan-Arab, pan-Islamic nature, such as those expressed by Gamal Abdel Nasser, Egypt's revered liberator and its President from 1956 to 1970. Significantly, Sa'ad Zaghlul, one of Egypt's greatest nationalist leaders and Prime Minister from 1924 to 1926, lies buried in a Cairo cemetery under a tomb shaped like a pharaonic temple.

In 1952, with the Revolution that ended the British Protectorate, Egypt came to be ruled by her own leaders for the first time since the Pharaohs. On the morning of July 26 in that year, King Faruq was put aboard the royal yacht and shipped off to Italy. It was perhaps symbolic that, when signing the instrument of abdication in Arabic, the corpulent, pleasure-loving monarch—Albanian-Turkish by descent—misspelt his own name; like most of his forebears, the Turkish viceroys, he had never bothered to master the Arabic language of the vast majority of his subjects, preferring instead to communicate in Turkish, French or English. He was followed into exile during the next few years—and particularly after the Suez crisis of 1956—by three quarters of a million Greeks, Italians, Syrians, Lebanese, Cypriots and Jews (collectively dubbed "Levantines" by the British) who made up the bulk of Egypt's permanent foreign community. The result was a temporary but massive dislocation of city life, as businesses, department stores, banks, hotels and restaurants lost not only their owners but also the people who supplied the managerial expertise.

Without the foreigners, Cairo became drabber and more chaotic but at least it belonged to the Egyptians. Mass urban migration—the worldwide phenomenon of the second half of the 20th Century—in Egypt invariably meant migration to Cairo. Millions of fellahin began flocking in from the countryside, placing ever-greater strains on Cairo's basic services, which had been installed before the Second World War to cope with a population of three million, as well as on a municipal authority that was already practically bankrupt. In the two or three years following 1967, the flood of newcomers was swollen by refugees from Port Sa'id, Isma'iliyah and Suez, the towns along the Suez Canal rendered virtually uninhabitable by Egypt's ruinously expensive war of attrition with Israel. Today, with a population of nine million—nearly a quarter of Egypt's total—Cairo is the largest city in Africa and the largest Islamic city in the world. It is still an open city and, if immigration continues at its present rate, the population will reach 15 million by 1990.

The influx of people has caused the city to explode outwards from its historic core in a flurry of new building. From the Cairo Tower, I had seen the suburb of 'Abbasiyah, its million flat-roofed houses stretching away north-east to the horizon, glimpsed the tower blocks of Nasr City, an ambitious high-density housing and commercial development reclaimed —with remarkable success—from the desert on the route out to Cairo's airport 13 miles away. On the west bank of the Nile, where at the beginning of the century the villages of Imbabah and Gizah lay among royal parks and farms, I had seen the same prospect of megalopolis, dominated by the huge, concrete offices sardonically known as "Nasser's Pyramids".

It took me many weeks before I felt I had come to any understanding of the different regions of the vast and complex city that now spreads away on all sides of the ancient centre—districts as different from each other as the leafy suburb of Ma'adi to the south, occupied by discreetly wealthy members of the middle classes and some foreign residents; the crumbling elegance of al-Sayyidah Zaynab, south-west of the Old City; and the neat

On waste land near a market in Cairo's southern outskirts, a tattooist works to a customer's specification beneath boards advertising a choice of ambitious designs. His portable kit has been improvised from an automobile battery. Tattooing—found on Egyptian mummies dating from about 2000 B.C.—was still practised by Cairenes during the 19th Century, but has lost its popularity among young people nowadays.

villas and apartment blocks of Madinat al-Muhandisin (Engineers' City) on the west bank, originally built to house the army officers and civil servants who formed the backbone of Nasser's regime.

But I began by finding my way around the city centre. My initial impression was of a nondescript international modernity. The broad boulevards were lined with offices, banks and stores—enlivened by an occasional de luxe cinema—and their pavements were crowded with shoppers and office workers, dressed for the most part in Western-style clothes that seemed drab in the glare of the Middle Eastern sun.

Around the official statues—pashas, generals, presidents—at the centres of major intersections swirled a noisy stream of traffic, among which I saw numerous expensive foreign cars, many of them scarred by exposure to the free-for-all of the Cairo streets. The shops I visited seemed to me agreeably old-fashioned; in place of the artfully lit window displays of Western department stores, they offered homely wooden counters piled high with merchandise. Most items on display—especially textiles and electrical equipment—were locally produced; in an effort to protect Egypt's young manufacturing industry, the government at that time still discouraged the import of consumer goods.

The very heart of Cairo is Tahrir Square, the site of the main bus station—and of the stately Egyptian Museum, built in the 1880s, which houses an unparalleled collection of antiquities, including the Tutankhamun treasure. Most of the square is given over to traffic, but the authorities have made one of their few concessions to pedestrians by erecting an elevated walkway circling the whole area. I stood there for perhaps an hour, observing the people crowding past me.

There can be no better place from which to observe the *mélange* of modern Egyptians. All the skin tones of the spectrum are in evidence, from the very black Sudanese immigrants from the south, through the hirsute, sallow-skinned Mediterranean and Levantine types, to the white-skinned Turko-Circassians, once the ruling class, but now a generally declining, impoverished élite. If there is a distinctively Egyptian type, it is to be found among the fellahin, the original inhabitants of the Nile valley, whose image can be seen on practically every ancient Egyptian wall-painting or relief. Slight and square-shouldered, with slim waists and slender limbs, they are among the most graceful people I know, having a casual fluidity of movement that is truly African. Many times, walking with Egyptians, I have felt like an ungainly northern barbarian, awkward and gauche.

Some of the newcomers who are swelling the city's population are bright young men who resent the limited horizons of provincial life and are drawn to the city in search of social and financial advancement. They soon become assimilated, adopting metropolitan ways and exchanging the *galabiyah* for Western-style clothes. But for the majority from the villages —the poor and landless who come to Cairo simply to seek a living—there is little difference between the city and the village. They feel no need to become urbanized, but have instead transplanted their own life to the city, a process that has invaded even the formerly "European" areas of the city.

A short walk northwards from the city centre showed me what was happening. In the business quarter of Bab al-Luq there are streets of stately apartment buildings, six or seven storeys high, designed around the turn of the century. The architects were mostly Italians, and Venetian Gothic windows, rococo plasterwork and Neapolitan-style wrought-iron balconies are much in evidence. I tried to imagine the typical sounds of these streets 50 years ago, when the inhabitants were probably wealthy Greek, Armenian and Jewish families: the rustle of long dresses, the tinkle of teacups, the murmur of polite conversation and the strains of a child practising the violin. Now, all was changed utterly. From a carpenter's basement shop came the whine of an electric saw, forcing the housewives in black country dresses to scream their gossip at each other from balconies festooned with laundry. In the rubbish-strewn street, a brown-fleeced ram, fattening for sacrifice on an approaching feast-day, was trying to extract some nutrition from a pile of wood shavings. On a doorstep a boy was tenderly picking lice from his little sister's hair.

Another example of Cairo's village life occurs on the rooftops. Viewed from above, some quarters of the city almost resemble an aerial farmyard. It is a regular rural practice to use the flat roofs of houses as an extra living space, but in Cairo it is taken one stage further; even on top of 19th-Century mansions, immigrants have built their mud-brick shacks high in

Outside a well-stocked butcher's shop in the wealthy district of Zamalik, a tethered sheep impassively awaits its fate. Government health regulations require that all meat sold over the counter in Cairo must be slaughtered at the civic abattoir; but to celebrate a special occasion—such as a wedding or a religious festival—many Cairene families still prefer to buy a live sheep or goat and slaughter it themselves at home.

the sky, where they lead their accustomed life, surrounded by their children, their poultry and, sometimes, even their goats.

The ancient district of Bulaq, lying immediately to the north of down-town Cairo, is one of the most densely settled in the city. History has dealt unkindly with Bulaq. Once an island caused by silting around a sunken boat, it merged with the east bank as the river gradually changed its course. From the 14th Century, Bulaq was Cairo's chief river port, a vital link in the spice trade with Europe; and the district retained its importance until the 19th Century, when it was chosen as the site of Egypt's earliest iron foundry, engineering college and gasworks. After that, its decline into overcrowded poverty was rapid and, since the Second World War, it has been swamped by rural immigrants.

I made my way down one of the main thoroughfares, observing all around me signs of the inhabitants' recent rustic origins: women in the customary dark-coloured, long-sleeved gowns, their heads covered with more or less intricately folded scarves; a large proportion of men in galabiyahs; goats and sheep tethered on odd patches of waste ground. Each little house—some of them concrete boxes of no great age, some made of the same kind of mud-bricks that Egyptians have used for centuries—was crammed with up to half a dozen families, living perhaps 10 to a room. Parts of Bulaq are said to have a staggering concentration of 300,000 people per square mile, 25 times the average density in London. The occupants seemed to accept as a matter of course an existence that offers them few material benefits beyond a roof over their heads and enough to eat; yet, I felt little of the sense of demoralization that usually goes with the word "slum".

Those who knew Cairo in its grander days may be appalled by the ubiquitous signs of squalor. Poverty is not a novel phenomenon, but before the mass migrations of recent years its manifestations were, at least in some districts, kept out of sight. The European quarters were reserved for Europeans and their streets were regularly swept. There is a story that one of King Faruq's sisters once said reprovingly to him: "Try to improve the living standards of your people. Whenever I come to visit you I have to pass through districts where conditions are quite dreadful."

"There's nothing I can do," replied the King, "and if the sight of the poor upsets you so much, close your eyes." Nowadays even the most aloof of Egyptian rulers would be hard put to ignore the poor.

By their sheer numbers, the poor of Cairo have completely altered the city's social balance. With their families and attendant animals they are everywhere, squatting in ancient tombs and mosques, raising their shacks on the roofs of rococo palaces, taking over derelict houseboats on the Nile. Their children dash at tourists and wealthier Egyptians alike, opening the doors of their cars at traffic-lights, ambushing them with flowers, plastic combs or chewing gum, or rushing to escort them from elevators—offering little services with confident insistence on a few small coins in return. They swamp public transport, clinging to the buffers of commuter trains or squatting on the roofs within perilous inches of the overhead electric cables.

True, foreigners and the Egyptian rich can still disport themselves in the grand style; there are now luxury hotels, with air-conditioning, private gardens and swimming pools, where a meal and a few drinks will cost what the average Egyptian labourer earns in a month. But for most of the city's inhabitants, these foreigners and the indigenous *haute bourgeoisie*, far from being the undisputed and envied lords of Cairo, are now little more than objects of curiosity and an occasional jest.

As my acquaintance with Cairo grew, I took to wandering about alone in all parts of the city. At first, as a fastidious European reared in quite different conventions, I was appalled by some of the sights I saw. A destitute woman pleaded for her sick child, a legless beggar exposed his stumps in the forecourt of a mosque, a blind man strode purposefully, arms outstretched, calling loudly for people to stand aside from his path.

But gradually I almost came to accept this as part of the natural order, as the philosophically disposed inhabitants apparently did, and to realize how much of my initial amazement was due to the special expectations with which I had arrived. Sorrow and fatigue were written on the faces of many Cairenes, but there was joy and excitement in the jaunty whistling of the errand boys on their battered bicycles and in the spontaneous laughter of the peasant girls riding by in donkey carts; there was vigour and life in the sudden shouting quarrels that would burst out at a moment's notice and disappear again in equally loud laughter. I realized that here poverty does not spell social failure, for the people do not necessarily see themselves as poor, in the material sense that implies deprivation; instead, the life they lead in the city is similar to the life they led in their villages, though with added complexities. I ceased to notice the crumbling buildings, the open sewers and the ubiquitous garbage, realizing that the special fascination of Cairo lies not in its glorious past, but in the vigour of its present inhabitants.

Tower blocks on Rawdah Island (centre) dwarf the Nilometer—a well with a central column marked at intervals to measure the river's level—built in A.D. 861 an‹

Relics of a Proud Past

…w capped with a modern conical turret. To the left of it stands the 19th-Century al-Monasterli palace, named after its builder, an adviser to Egypt's Ottoman rulers.

Cairo has dominated the Nile for more than 10 centuries, yet some three quarters of its 120-square-mile area is less than a century old. Seen from the air, much of the city presents an almost uniform vista of 20th-Century development; but on the Nile's east bank (on the right, above)—site of the city's ancestral settlements—and on two long islands that lie in midstream, the profusion of modern buildings is punctuated by abrupt juxtapositions of mosques, cemeteries and fortifications dating from the city's earlier epochs. Cairo's first Islamic settlements were enlarged by a succession of later rulers—Arab, Turkish and European—all of whom left the mark of their own styles of architecture upon the growing city. Although many landmarks have been submerged by the wave of 20th-Century expansion, enough remain to recall the strata underlying today's city.

In the Old City, parked cars choke a square flanked by two ancient mosques. The courtyard with arched cloisters (background, left) belongs to al-Azhar, a religio

oundation harbouring a thousand-year-old university; the dome and stumpy minaret (foreground, right) are part of the Sayyidna al-Husayn mosque, founded in 1154.

Densely clustered high-rise buildings (background) contrast with the spacious formality of a medieval cemetery at Cairo's eastern limit. The neat streets enhanc

he effect of the uncannily lifelike homes for the dead. Many of the one-storey tombs are occupied by squatters who cannot find other homes in overcrowded Cairo.

Beyond the confluence of two broad streets in north-eastern Cairo—Shari' Port Sa'id (left) and Shari' al-Gaysh—tenements erected to cope with the 20th-Centur

flux of peasants into the city surround a lone stand of trees (top, centre) that marks the 13th-Century mosque built for Sultan al-Baybars, a Mamluk ruler of Egypt.

At the city's south-eastern edge, a sturdy rampart—added by the Ottoman Turks to the original Citadel (far right) built in the 12th Century by the Sultan Saladir

...ovides the foundation for a prominent Cairo landmark: the domes and slender minarets of the mosque begun in 1824 by the Ottoman Pasha Muhammad 'Ali.

2

An Ancient Heart

The successive Persian, Roman and early Islamic settlements that once stood in the area covered by modern Cairo long ago crumbled to dust, but the Old City, the descendant of al-Qahirah, has endured for a thousand years. Its extent is less than one square mile, but it contains more recorded ancient monuments—mosques, tombs, private dwellings and caravan-serais—than any other African or Middle Eastern city. From the Cairo Tower, I had seen the Old City as a broad swathe of brown and ochre running north and south behind the grey of today's metropolis, and so I soon decided to spend a whole day exploring it and identifying the more notable of its hundreds of historic buildings. I knew that the district was not the equivalent of Rome's Forum or Athens' Acropolis—a lovingly pre-served memorial of a vanished, glorious age. Even so, I was not prepared for the scuffed and down-at-the-heel appearance presented by Cairo's ancient heart, or the scant respect with which it was treated by its present occupants. I was to find, however, that the Old City has a welcome attribute that is lacking in most other monuments: a living, human presence.

The Old City of today is still surrounded by considerable stretches of the ancient walls that once defended it, and I started my exploration at the northern perimeter, where the 11th-Century Bab al-Futuh (Gate of Conquests) leads into the Shari' al-Mu'izz, a north-south thoroughfare running the length of the Old City.

Flanking the broad archway of the Bab al-Futuh are two severe, rounded towers, 65 feet high. They were—after the Pyramids—the most solid-looking pieces of masonry I had so far seen in Cairo. Across the open space in front of them sprawled an untidy vegetable and fruit market, loud with the sound of bargaining and redolent with the smell of onions and garlic—it is the main garlic market for the whole of Cairo. The rickety wooden stalls and carts, shaded by large umbrellas, were piled with watermelons, cauliflowers, tomatoes, aubergines and lemons that had been brought in by peasants from outlying villages all around Cairo.

I followed the steady stream of traffic—two-legged, four-legged and wheeled—that pushed and jostled its way through the Bab al-Futuh, and stepped aside to admire the flawless masonry. As I did so, the custodian of the gateway materialized at my elbow and offered to show me around the interior. As we went up its narrow spiral staircase, I noticed in the walls fragments of pink granite bearing hieroglyphic inscriptions, and even a charming relief of a hippopotamus—re-used relics from some pharaonic building. We eventually emerged on to the city ramparts, where

The exquisite workmanship of this 12th-Century lustreware bowl, featuring a young nobleman hunting with a hawk, testifies to the artistic achievements and courtly life of Cairo under the Fatimid dynasty. The Fatimids—so-called because they claimed direct descent from the prophet Muhammad's daughter Fatimah—ruled Egypt between 969 and 1171 from their palace-city of al-Qahirah, whose site is today covered by the Old City, Cairo's medieval core.

after a few yards' stroll along the wall another evocative detail appeared: a smaller medieval tower with the words TOUR MILHAUD carved over its doorway. Milhaud, I later learnt, was one of the aides-de-camp who had accompanied Napoleon Bonaparte on his brief and ill-fated military expedition to Egypt in 1798, and had helped to oversee the repairs the French made to Cairo's fortifications.

Back at the foot of the Bab al-Futuh, I found myself in a dusty, sunlit square dotted with people and donkeys. Several carts with massive six-foot-diameter wheels were propped against the walls. Along one side of the square stretched a row of two-storey houses made of mud-brick, a material that lasts well in Egypt's dry climate, where rainfall is a desultory one inch a year. Even so, the ingenious patching of mud and timber visible on many of their walls showed me that the houses were far from indestructible. At intervals—perhaps where an especially disastrous collapse had taken place—the terrace was interrupted by modern concrete dwellings four or five storeys high of an angular, jerry-built sort. Coated in the omnipresent dust of Cairo that is constantly blown in from the desert, they looked scarcely newer than their scruffy neighbours.

Across the square was a startling architectural contrast: the crenellated walls and block-like angle towers of the huge mosque built by al-Hakim, the Fatimid Caliph of al-Qahirah who ruled from A.D. 996 until 1021. The Fatimids, so-called because they claimed to be descended from the prophet Muhammad through his daughter Fatimah, were a dynasty of rulers who established themselves in Egypt by conquest in 969, more than three centuries after the first Arab invasion had claimed Egypt for Islam in 641. They belonged to the Shi'ah, a dissident Muslim faction that believed the leadership of Islam should forever reside with the descendants of 'Ali, Muhammad's cousin and Fatimah's husband, who had been assassinated in 661. The Shi'ah claimed to possess an esoteric body of knowledge communicated to 'Ali by the Prophet himself and handed down through a line of hereditary leaders, or Imams, whose word was considered absolute and infallible. By contrast, the majority faction within Islam, the Sunni (the name comes from the word *sunnah*, meaning "well-trodden path"), believed in rule by consensus. They maintained that the caliph, the "successor" of the Prophet, should be chosen not by heredity but by the acclamation of the people—in practice, usually by the *'ulama'*, the body of lawyers entrusted with interpreting the Koran. Ever since 'Ali's death, the Sunni cause—represented by the caliphate of Damascus and later Baghdad—had been politically in the ascendant, and the Shi'ites had been in the minority. The schism still persists in the Islamic world.

For security, the Fatimids built al-Qahirah two miles north of the earlier and still-flourishing town of al-Fustat, where the new city would catch the prevailing cool northerly breezes, and would avoid the smell from the rubbish tips that consequently built up to the south side of any settlement.

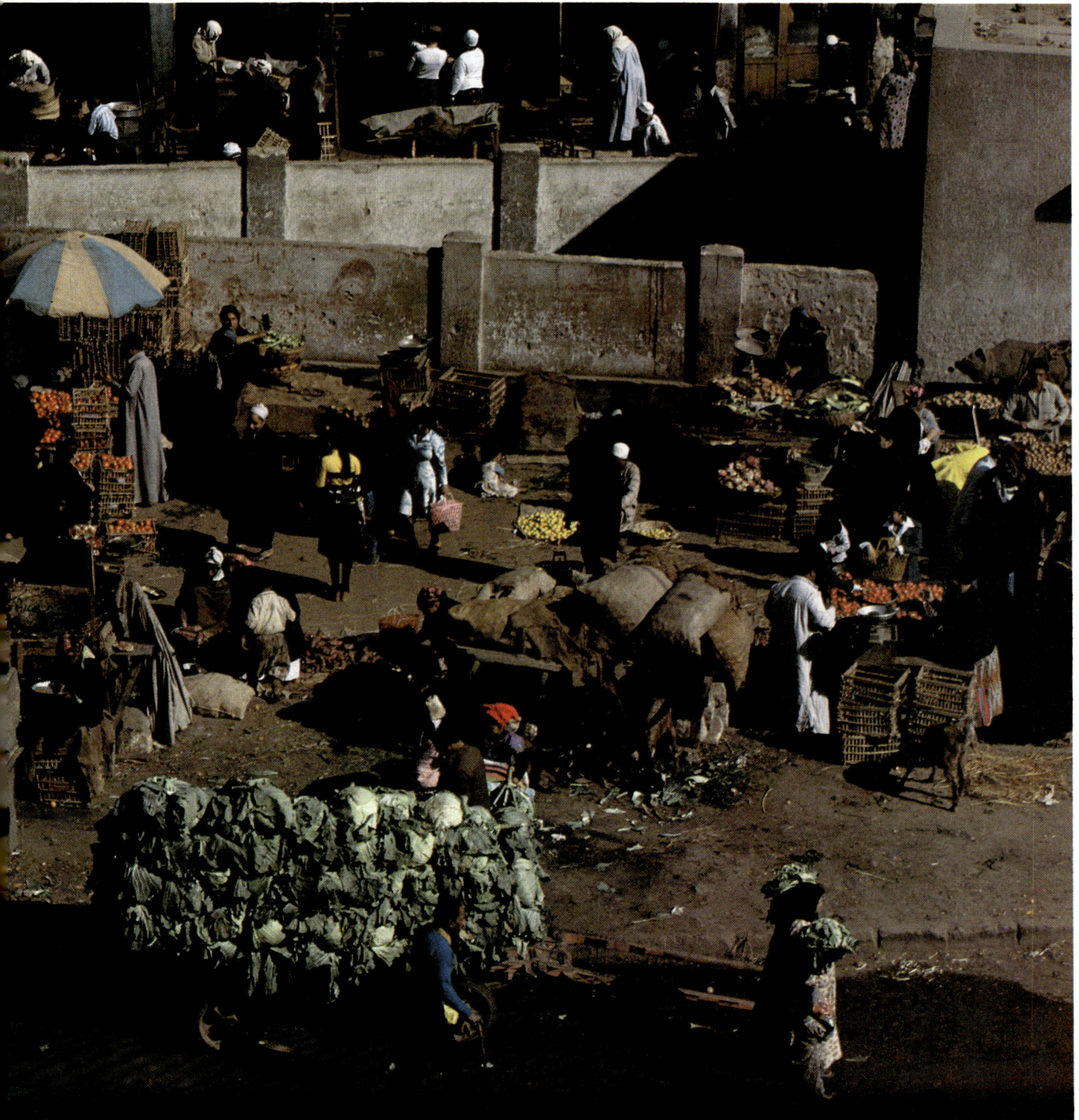

In a market at the northern edge of the Old City, fruit and vegetables brought in daily from the Nile Delta's fertile farmlands are sold to Cairo's inhabitants.

The Fatimid foundation was a closed palace-city covering almost half a square mile, containing within its walls two immense palaces and their gardens, several beautiful mosques and a university. Only the rulers and their retinue lived in al-Qahirah; in the 11th Century, the total number of inmates of the palace—including officials, concubines and slaves—was estimated at 30,000. The much greater number of ordinary townspeople lived outside the walls or in al-Fustat.

Al-Hakim, builder of the mosque I stood before, was one of the ogres of Egyptian history—at least according to hostile Christian sources. Like all Fatimid rulers, he considered himself the Imam, a leader divinely appointed by God (his Egyptian subjects, who remained Sunni, disagreed); and he allowed himself unbounded freedom to do, say or think what he liked. On the evidence of the historical record, al-Hakim was clearly mad. His staring blue eyes frightened all those who looked at him. As one of his lighter diversions, he would ride around the city late at night, ordering the people to open their shops and re-light the street-lamps to encourage activity and gaiety, but as soon as they began to enjoy themselves, he would send them home again. More in character was his alleged habit of buying slave children, playing with them for a while, and then disembowelling them with his own hands. Ultimately, the mad Caliph had the effrontery to proclaim himself God Incarnate, and alienated his subjects still further. His end was mysterious; one day in 1021 he disappeared somewhere in the Muqattam Hills, where he was in the habit of riding about alone on a white donkey.

I wandered into al-Hakim's mosque and gazed around. Although the largest of the surviving Fatimid monuments, it has received little respect throughout the years. In the 13th Century it was used as a stable; Napoleon converted it into a military storehouse. Today, it has been partially restored, although the brick arcades surrounding its huge open courtyard are still roofless. When I was there, the only other occupants of the place were a few little boys in *galabiyahs* playing football; the mosque is now a primary school, with the courtyard serving as its playground.

The Fatimids' reign lasted for two centuries, during which their city became an important centre of learning and commerce. Because their Shi'ite heritage precluded relations with Baghdad and other centres of Sunni Islam, the Fatimids looked to the West and the Christian world. They traded with Italian merchants and with Constantinople, capital of the Byzantine Empire; employed large numbers of Christians as administrators; and in the 12th Century even concluded a temporary alliance with the Crusaders, who had begun to infiltrate Palestine.

In 1168 Amalric, the French nobleman who ruled the Crusader kingdom of Jerusalem, sent his knights, Hugh of Caesarea and Geoffrey Fulcher, to discuss the terms of the pact with the 16-year-old Fatimid Caliph, al-'Adid. The chronicler William of Tyre described the sumptuous welcome

TheTides of Time

B.C. c. 5000	First farming settlements develop in the Nile valley
c. 3500	Two kingdoms emerge: Upper Egypt in the Nile valley and Lower Egypt in the Delta, to the north
c. 3100	Upper and Lower Egypt unite under Pharaohs, with royal capital at Memphis, 20 miles south of present-day Cairo
c. 2700-2300	Numerous stone pyramids built in Nile valley, the earliest being the Step Pyramid at Saqqarah, the cemetery of Memphis
c. 2600-2500	Three great Pyramids and the Sphinx completed by Pharaoh Khufu and his successors at Gizah, nine miles south-west of present-day Cairo
c. 2400	Thebes, 450 miles south of modern Cairo, becomes capital of Egypt, eclipsing Memphis
525	Persian invaders incorporate Egypt into their empire. On a site now part of city's southern suburbs, they build fortress of Babylon to guard Nile crossing
332	Alexander the Great conquers Persian Empire—including Egypt—and founds a new Egyptian capital, Alexandria, on the coast. After Alexander's death, Ptolemy—one of his generals—establishes Greek-speaking dynasty
30	Octavian (later to become Emperor Augustus) defeats Queen Cleopatra, last of the Ptolemies, and annexes Egypt to the Roman Empire
A.D. 1st Century	Christianity reaches Egypt
130	New Roman fortress is built at Babylon, by now developing into a flourishing trading community
451	The Copts, Egypt's Christians, declared heretics by the Roman Church
622	Prophet Muhammad establishes first Islamic community at al-Madinah in Arabia
632	Death of Muhammad. Muslim power spreads rapidly under rule of caliphs (successors of the Prophet)
641	Muslim armies conquer Egypt and found new capital, al-Fustat, beside fortress of Babylon. Islam becomes official religion
661	Islam splits into Sunni and Shi'ah branches. Ummayad caliphs rule Egypt from Damascus
750	'Abbasid caliphs of Baghdad gain leadership of Islamic world, take over Egypt and build new palace city, al-'Askar, just north-east of al-Fustat
868	Ibn Tulun, a general sent by the 'Abbasids to govern Egypt, assumes absolute power and founds his own palace-city, al-Qata'l', north of al-Fustat and al-'Askar
878	Mosque of Ibn Tulun is completed
969	Fatimids, a Shi'ite dynasty from Tunisia, invade Egypt and found new palace-city of al-Qahirah (Cairo) north of al-'Askar and al-Qata'l'—which have already been absorbed by al-Fustat
971	Mosque and theological college of al-Azhar founded
1010	Mosque of Sultan al-Hakim completed
1099	European armies of First Crusade capture Jerusalem from Muslims
1168	Al-Fustat largely razed by fire to prevent occupation by armies of the Second Crusade
1171	Fatimid dynasty dies out. Saladin, a Kurdish soldier defending Egypt from Crusaders, seizes power. Sunni Islam restored
1175	Construction of Cairo's Citadel begins and city fortifications extended
1250	The Mamluks—a military élite of freed slaves—usurp the sultanate from Saladin's dynasty
1250-1517	Under a succession of 48 Mamluk sultans, Cairo grows into one of the world's richest commercial cities, with estimated population of 500,000. Mamluks endow it with dozens of superb buildings
1498	Discovery of Cape sea route from Europe to the Far East destroys Egypt's domination of overland trade
1517	Ottoman Turks conquer Egypt and transform it into a province of their empire
1517-1798	Under negligent rule of Ottoman viceroys, Mamluks regain their power and cause political chaos by their feuding. Egypt suffers economic and cultural recession; Cairo's population falls to 300,000
1798	To block Britain's trade routes to India, Napoleon Bonaparte invades Egypt. He brings scholars with him to study Egyptian history and culture

that the Crusader delegation received, in an account summarized by the 19th-Century historian Stanley Lane-Poole: "The wezir [minister] himself conducted them with every detail of oriental ceremony and display to the Great Palace of the Fatimids. They were led by mysterious corridors and through guarded doors, where stalwart Sudanis saluted with naked swords. They reached a spacious court, open to the sky and surrounded by arcades resting on marble pillars; the panelled ceilings were carved and inlaid in gold and colours; the pavement was rich mosaic. The unaccustomed eyes of the rude knights opened wide with wonder at the taste and refinement that met them at every step; here they saw marble fountains, birds of many notes and wondrous plumage, strangers to the western world."

The Fatimids were supplanted by Salah al-Din—known to the West as Saladin, the gallant soldier who recaptured Jerusalem from the Crusaders. Of Kurdish birth, he originally came to Egypt with his uncle—a general in the service of the Zengid Turks of Syria—who had been sent to ward off a Crusader invasion. But Saladin stayed on, and when the last Fatimid Caliph died in 1171 he made himself Sultan of Egypt in his own right.

As a Sunni, Saladin sought to extirpate the dangerous Shi'ah doctrines of his predecessors by founding the first Cairo *madrasah*—a theological college for the study and interpretation of the Koran and Islamic law. He threw open the gates of al-Qahirah to the common people and built the massive Citadel that still frowns down on the Old City from a rocky ledge of the Muqattam Hills to the south-east. The fortress was garrisoned by a succession of later conquerors and is still used as a military barracks.

Leaving al-Hakim's mosque—which Saladin had used as a prison camp for captured Crusaders—I resumed my southerly course down the Shari' al-Mu'izz. The hectic bustle of the Old City pressed in on me. I collided with men carrying rolls of cloth or trays of sweetmeats on their heads and tried to avoid small children in cotton pyjamas who darted amongst the forest of adult legs. In spite of the crush of humanity, a stream of animals and wheeled traffic—including donkeys which were almost invisible under their load of vegetables, and handcarts piled with cardboard boxes or live poultry in flimsy cages made from sugar-cane, secured precariously with bits of string—managed to force their passage. The cart-pullers and animal-drivers served warning of their approach by emitting a penetrating snake-like hiss; uttered suddenly, often within an inch of my ear, the sound was curiously disturbing. Incredibly, motor traffic was also allowed to use the congested thoroughfare, which was originally designed in Fatimid times, it is said, to accommodate no more than two laden pack animals abreast. Youths on motorbikes, as well as battered old taxis and trucks, blared their way arrogantly through the crowd, scattering humble pedestrians in all directions.

My progress was slow and hazardous. If I stuck to the side of the street, I had to brave the smiling importunities of the shopkeepers, who insistently asked that I come inside and view their wares, or at least stop for a cup of coffee. Escape to the middle of the road seemed equally pointless, not only because of the relentless traffic, but also because of the reeking pools of water that had overflowed from the sewers. Since the completion of the Aswan High Dam, the water table in Cairo has risen appreciably, causing the city's antiquated drainage system literally to crack under the strain.

Curiously enough, as I fought my way through the multitude I felt my initial claustrophobia ebbing away. The crowd density encountered in the streets of the Old City is easily as great as that of the London rush hour, yet the response of the participants is vastly different: where the British tend to adopt a frigid stoicism, the Cairenes retain an extrovert good humour that is ultimately reassuring.

The dynasty founded by Saladin lasted less than a century. By the middle of the 13th Century a new kind of ruler had come to power in Cairo. These were the Mamluks, war-lords who held power from 1250 until 1517, when Egypt was overrun by the Ottoman Turks and reduced to the status of a mere province of their empire. It was during the period of the Mamluks' rule that many of the most beautiful of Cairo's buildings were erected, particularly along the ancient course of Shari' al-Mu'izz. The domes with which the sultans crowned their grandiose tombs, flanked by extravagant, multi-tiered minarets, are to this day one of the most pleasing and characteristic sights of the Old City.

The word "mamluk" means "one who is owned" and gives a clue to the extraordinary background of the new élite. By origin they were male slaves—mainly of Turkish or Mongol stock from the steppes of central Asia, or Circassians from the Caucasus—who had been captured or purchased from their parents at about the age of 10 and brought to Egypt to be trained as palace guards. Their rootlessness, and the fact that they were eventually rewarded by being given their freedom, was supposed to ensure disinterested loyalty. The custom had begun in 9th-Century Baghdad, and eventually spread throughout the Muslim world, from Afghanistan to Spain. Equally widespread, however, was the tendency of these palace guards to take advantage of an indolent ruler and gather political power into their own hands.

By the middle of the 13th Century, the Mamluks of Egypt had become the most powerful faction in the land, holding high command in the army and occupying large country estates as a reward for their services. When, in 1250, the short-lived dynasty founded by Saladin came to an end, the Mamluks took over the country. During the next 50 years, their armies cleared the remnants of the Crusaders out of the Levant, checked the westward advance of the fearsome Mongol hordes into Syria and Palestine, and carved out an empire that extended northwards as far as eastern Turkey. Cairo, the Mamluk capital, became the largest city in the world,

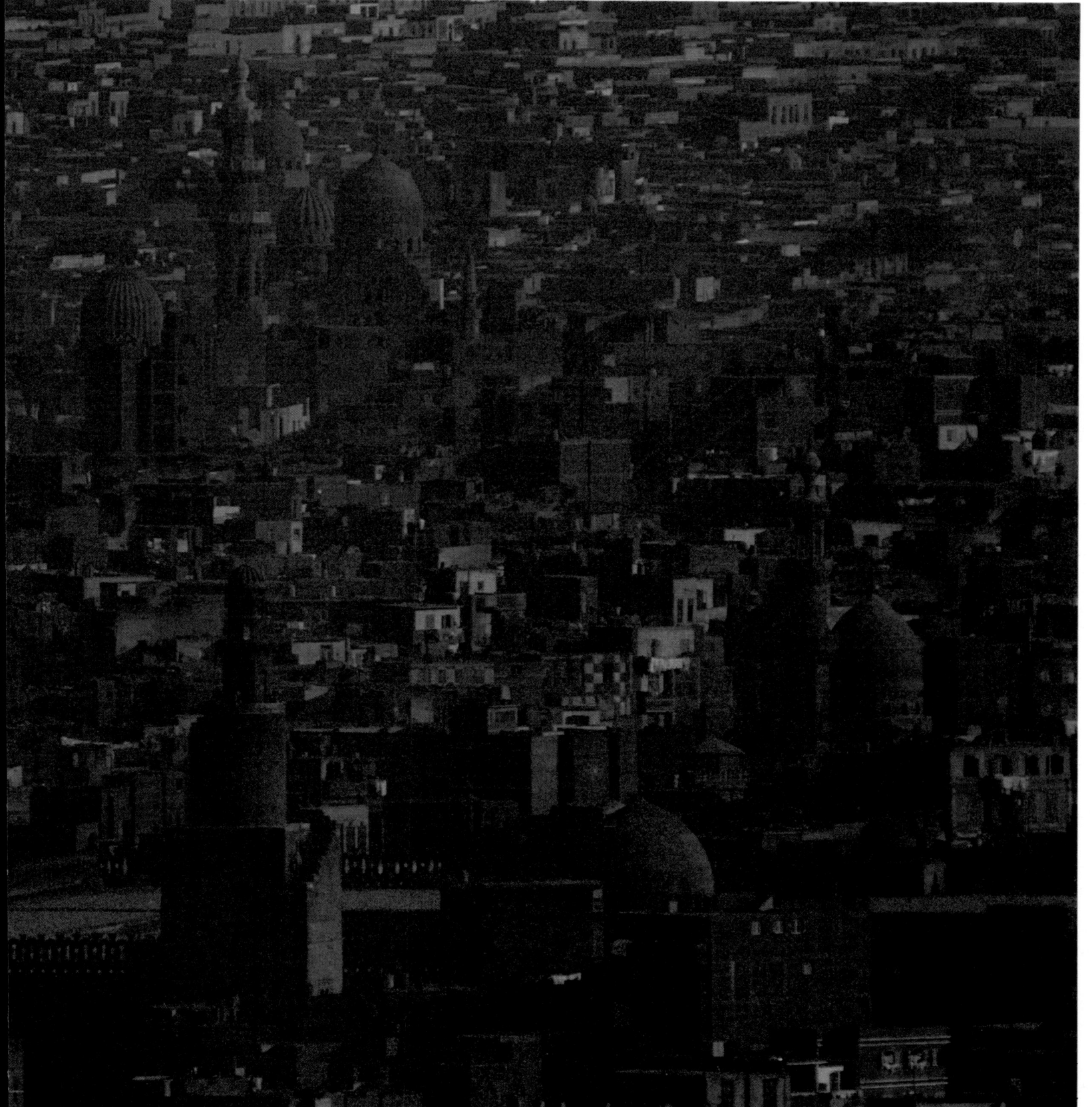

Among domes of later ages, a sturdy minaret (foreground, centre) marks the austerely beautiful mosque built by Ibn Tulun, a 9th-Century ruler of Egypt.

with half a million inhabitants, and a leading centre of economic, political and cultural life in the Middle East.

Through the city's busy warehouses passed precious shipments of silk and spices from India, China and the Indonesian archipelago, en route to the markets of Constantinople and Venice; the medieval Egyptian topographer al-Maqrizi estimated that in the early 14th Century the city contained 35 major markets and no fewer than 20,000 shops. Under Mamluk patronage, the city experienced a remarkable flowering of science and the arts. Advanced medical research, into such subjects as eye disease, the circulation of the blood and veterinary surgery, was carried out. Historical writing flourished: the *Muqaddimah*, the introduction to a history of the Muslim world produced in the late 14th Century by Ibn Khaldun, is considered to be the earliest treatise to take into account not only the moral and intellectual forces that affect the history of mankind, but also the material factors, such as climate, geography and trade.

But Mamluk rule also had its negative side. Each sultan was usually elected by the "acclamation" of his own particular group of supporters— after all his most dangerous rivals had been killed during fierce infighting. Since the new sultan was, in turn, likely to be assassinated and his offspring cast adrift, the principle of peaceful hereditary succession was hardly ever put into practice. Of the 48 Mamluk sultans, only one managed to found a dynasty that lasted three generations.

The Mamluks were a paradox. They could be unimaginably cruel to their own kind—defeated claimants to power were sometimes nailed to a plank and paraded through the streets on the back of a donkey—yet they were also genuinely pious. Inspired by the ardour of the newly converted— after their arrival in Egypt they were brought up as Muslims—and perhaps the desire to legitimize their regime, successive sultans tried to improve the moral tone of Cairo by closing down brothels and banning alcohol, and by enriching the city with dozens of mosques, *madrasahs* and tombs.

The skyline of the Shari' al-Mu'izz is one of the best-preserved monuments to Mamluk piety. As I walked along the thoroughfare I found on my left, rising serenely above the honking traffic and the din of commerce, a stately sequence of buildings, their façades, domes and minarets still magnificent despite their battered condition. I passed the delicately detailed *madrasah* founded in 1386 by the Sultan Barquq, and beyond it, one built by an earlier ruler, al-Nasir, foremost of the Mamluk builders in Cairo. During his long reign from 1293 to 1340, al-Nasir is said to have endowed the city with 30 mosques, an aqueduct and a canal. Only the shell remains of his *madrasah* on the Shari' al-Mu'izz, but I paused to admire its Gothic doorway, looted from a Crusader church in Acre.

A few steps further down the street, I came to the great 13th-Century foundation of the Sultan Qala'un, a complex of buildings that originally included a *madrasah*, a mausoleum and a *maristan*, or hospital. Qala'un, father of al-Nasir, was a handsome, broad-shouldered man who had been bought as a slave for the unusually high price of a thousand gold dinars, and eventually had the good fortune to be acclaimed Sultan in 1279. The lofty battlemented façade of his splendid group of sacred and secular buildings has pointed arches that led my eye upwards to a smooth, egg-shaped dome and sturdy minaret—a vision that triumphed effortlessly over the cramped surroundings.

Passing through the main portal and down a broad corridor, I turned right into a high, quiet, airy room, its ceiling supported by massive columns and its walls glowing with marble and mosaics. This was the mausoleum of the Sultan himself whose body, together with that of al-Nasir, lay within a gabled wooden tomb screened by a carved wooden grille in the centre of the room. Behind the mausoleum, I sought out a neglected courtyard—all that survives of the hospital of Qala'un, once the marvel of its age and in use until the 1850s. All ailments were treated there free of charge by specialists, and there were separate wards for each disease—for the Arabs knew about the risks of contagion long before the West. The patients were even entertained during their stay by musicians and story-tellers.

The third component of the ancient foundation is a *madrasah*, in this case a great court with two colonnaded halls, one at either end. It is in an appalling state of repair, but must once have been as magnificent as the neighbouring mausoleum. When I was there, it was sheltering several families who had been housed there, probably because their previous dwellings had collapsed—an all-too-frequent occurrence in Cairo—or otherwise become uninhabitable. To ensure a little privacy, they had erected crude wood and cloth partitions in the covered sanctuary area, nailing rough timbers directly into the delicate stucco of the walls. They lived surrounded by their bedding, their pots and pans and their livestock. Goats, chickens and grubby children were wandering about, performing their natural functions at will—although there were also some neatly dressed schoolgirls, and behind the rough awnings I caught sight of at least one flickering television set.

Qala'un's dynasty represents Mamluk Egypt at the zenith of its vigour and prosperity; less than 50 years after his son al-Nasir completed the mausoleum in 1293, decline had set in. The later sultans were as tyrannical as they had ever been, but no longer possessed the redeeming virtues of being competent rulers. Their extortionate taxes and their vicious quarrelling amongst themselves undermined the nation's economy and demoralized the people. But the Mamluks still went on building; indeed, it almost seemed that the faster the darkness gathered over Egypt, the more splendid her architecture became. Perhaps the most sophisticated building still standing in Cairo is the mausoleum in the nearby Northern Cemetery built for the Sultan Qa'it Bay in 1472, only 45 years before the final destruction of the Mamluk kingdom in 1517 by the Ottoman Sultan

A 16th-Century dome demonstrates the full flowering of arabesque decoration.

Eye-dazzling chevrons clothe a mid-15th-Century dome.

Domes of Intricate Detail

Of the scores of domes that grace Cairo's skyline, the most ornate were erected over the tombs of Mamluks, members of the military caste that ruled Egypt from 1250 to 1517. Built of soft, local limestone, the domes lent themselves to increasingly brilliant carved decoration; beginning with simple, vertical ribbing, Cairo's stonemasons soon introduced fluent chevron patterns, and finally developed arabesque designs of astonishing beauty.

leaf pattern dates from the late 15th Century.

mple 14th-Century ribbing gives a bold effect.

Selim the Grim. Its dome of soft limestone is carved with a brilliant, hard-edged pattern of interlocking stars that weaves in and out of an undulating lacework of leaf-like arabesques, like a fugue in two contrasting voices. This wonderful tomb commemorates a ruler renowned both for extravagant spending and for violence, who gave Cairo many splendid buildings yet is alleged to have torn out the eyes and tongue of one of his alchemists because he failed to turn base metal into gold.

In a precarious and hard-driven way, the Old City preserves some of the activities as well as the fabric of its history. It is a separate and identifiable district, where the rural echoes that have become increasingly common in other quarters are less noticeable because of the centuries of urban life that lie behind it. Roughly the same number of people—about half a million—live in the Old City as were there in Mamluk times. Only two recent streets slice through its alley-ways to connect it with the modern city half a mile away: one is the Shari' Gawhar al-Qa'id, completed in the 19th Century by Isma'il; and the other is the Shari' al-Azhar, laid out in the 1920s. The patched tarmac, clattering trams and nondescript fringe of department stores and office blocks of these later thoroughfares seem to belong to a world different from that of the alleys and dead-end lanes of the great bazaar area that still occupies the heart of the Old City.

The din of nearby hammering told me that I was approaching the *suq*, or market, of the metalworkers. It is located on the edge of the bazaar area, a bewildering warren of narrow alley-ways lined with hundreds of little stalls offering every kind of merchandise, from luxury goods, such as lapis lazuli and gold, to more mundane items such as plastic cups, sandals, clothing, batteries, watches and vegetables. This bazaar quarter of Cairo cannot have changed very much since the days when the great camel caravans used to arrive along the desert trails from Syria or the Sudan. As in medieval times, each type of commodity is sold in its own special area, many of which betray their location by their distinctive fragrance. A pleasantly musty smell drew me to the textile market, piled with rolls of cotton and silk that the salesmen were energetically unrolling across the counter in order to demonstrate their merits to prospective buyers. The rich odour of attar and sandalwood heralded the perfume *suq*, with its rows of small bottles containing oils pressed from dozens of different kinds of flowers. There I saw a vignette that might have been familiar 600 years ago: an old gentleman in a blue *galabiyah* cautiously sniffing at the samples.

Among the stalls selling spices—the commodity upon which medieval Cairo grew rich, until the Portuguese discovered the sea route to the East in 1492 and undermined the Egyptian monopoly—I saw sack after sack of cumin, saffron, coriander, ginger and cardamom, together with dried herbs and flowers for tisanes, and walnuts and hazelnuts, imported luxuries eaten at religious festivals. Located at the centre of the bazaars, for reasons of security, is the gold and silver *suq*, which sells some tourist

trinkets, but mostly the chains, bracelets and coins that go to make up the dowry of many Egyptian girls. Gold is still the primary form of investment for village families, but it is worn rather than hoarded away in strong-rooms.

Exploring the bazaars, I realized how perfectly the layout of the Old City was adapted to the functions of a medieval trading centre, established to fulfil the particular requirements of merchants who had transported their goods from afar. Central to the arrangement were the *suqs*, where the merchandise was exchanged. Conveniently near were mosques, where the merchants could pray—and sometimes discuss business. Islam recognizes no distinction between religious and secular functions; mosques were used not only as places of prayer but also as schools, hostels for wayfarers and community centres.

A third essential institution of the medieval city was the *wakalah*: in these great caravanserais, the merchants could store their goods and also get room and board for the duration of their stay in the city. One of my pleasantest visits was to a *wakalah* that survives, though much-restored, in the southern half of the bazaar area. Around its courtyard, which has a refreshing fountain in the middle, there are tiny shops and above them three storeys of rooms for lodgings. Compared with the hectic streets outside, the *wakalah* was quiet and cool; once, however, it must have rung with emphatic bargaining, just as the bazaars do today.

A less attractive use for such a building can be seen a few blocks to the east of the Shari' al-Mu'izz. The Khan al-Khalili—once a 14th-Century caravanserai, now a covered *suq*—has become one of the few places in

Two of Cairo's crowded buses—one carrying a young hanger-on—edge past each other in the Shari' Bab al-Wazir, one of the broader thoroughfares bordering the medieval city. Most of the streets in Cairo's older quarters, originally built to accommodate only animal and pedestrian traffic, are too narrow for the passage of even a single modern vehicle.

the Old City that is firmly on the tourist track. The Germans, Americans and Britons who arrive for package holidays of seven or 14 days are piled into air-conditioned motor coaches and whisked around a few of the "acceptable" Cairo sights: the Pyramids, of course; the Citadel; the beautiful 14th-Century *madrasah* of Sultan Hassan; perhaps a Coptic church in the southern suburb of Misr al-Qadimah—and, invariably, the Khan al-Khalili. I noticed that, in contrast to those in the Shari' al-Mu'izz, the shops here were clean and smart and often had plate-glass windows and neon signs. They sold a curious mixture of hideous "oriental" souvenirs—including plaster models of the Sphinx—rather dubious antiquities and pleasant local handicrafts such as decorated leather, engraved brass bowls, mother-of-pearl inlay work and carpets. Needless to say, the prices were heavily inflated; I later saw many of the same goods on sale elsewhere in Cairo at a quarter of the price.

The place was crowded with foreign visitors who wore the glazed expression of people who do not quite know why they are where they are, and the shopkeepers demonstrated the ingratiating manner that comes from prolonged contact with the tourist milch cow. I made a mental note to avoid the Khan al-Khalili in future.

Later in the day, in one of the streets to the north, I came across an elegant façade, distinguished by rows of projecting wooden balconies enclosed by delicate lattice screens. This was the 17th-Century Bayt al-Sihaymi, a fine example of the traditional family mansions that were built throughout the Old City in Mamluk and, later, in Ottoman times, right up to the 19th Century. These Cairo houses are among the most underestimated achievements of Egyptian civilization and the indifference with which they are now treated is nothing short of tragic. Only a handful have been preserved and the remainder are crumbling rapidly under the pressure of occupation by squatters.

The central feature of the Bayt al-Sihaymi is a spacious *qa'ah*, or chief reception room, two floors in height and lit by a raised section of roof that accommodates extra windows. Fresh air is kept in circulation by a *malqaf*—a shaft that rises through the roof and has an inlet angled to catch the prevailing northerly breezes. Even if there is no perceptible wind, hot air rises out of the raised vents and is replaced by cooler air drawn in from the *malqaf*. I saw the house on a particularly hot day, but the temperature drop in the *qa'ah* was little less than that produced by the sophisticated air-conditioning at my hotel. A primitive form of *malqaf* is featured on wall-paintings of the second millennium B.C. at Thebes, suggesting that the 17th-Century version I saw already had the benefit of about 30 centuries of technical improvement.

Around the *qa'ah* are slightly raised seating areas known as *liwans*, with elaborate semi-domed ceilings enclosed by arches. Overlooking the room from the adjoining harem area are the wooden *mashrabiyah* windows, a striking feature of Cairo architecture, through which the women of the household could peer at what was going on, without themselves being seen. These latticed screens, made up of innumerable tiny pieces of turned wood in an intricate design, minimize the sun's glare and allow for the maximum circulation of air. I looked through a *mashrabiyah*, and the palms and mimosas in the garden outside were reduced to two-dimensional patterns, like a piece of embroidery.

The most attractive part of the Bayt al-Sihaymi is the harem area, which overlooks the tranquil inner court. The coolness of its upstairs *qa'ah* is beautifully enhanced by the blue and white glazed Turkish tiles on its walls. From another room, as I looked out through a *mashrabiyah* into the street outside, I caught sight of two coppersmiths in the workshop across the way, beating patterns into a tray. One held the tray, turning it in his hands, while the other wielded his hammer with a regular, musical rhythm; the co-ordination between them was instinctive, the product of long years of practice. On the roof of the same workshop a dyer had spread out his brightly coloured cottons to dry.

During my early wanderings in the Old City I had been struck by the large number of magnificent and ancient buildings that were being put to the most mundane uses, officially or unofficially. It was an impression that was strengthened as the day went on. To add to the other examples I had encountered, there were the *madrasah* and mausoleum built—facing each other across the Shari' al-Mu'izz—by Qansuh al-Ghawri, the next-to-last Mamluk Sultan, who died fighting the Ottoman Turks in 1516. The chief attraction of his *madrasah* is its minaret, crowned with five rather frivolous little finials. Qansuh al-Ghawri's body was never found, but his mausoleum received the bodies of various relatives and his successor. I looked inside briefly; the dome of the great vaulted chamber originally prepared for the Sultan's tomb has collapsed and the hall is now fitted out as a basketball court, occasionally doubling as a cinema; for the building is now a community centre that provides evening classes for adults, as well as workshops for artists. The use might seem incongruous, but at least the building was in good repair. I also saw fine buildings summarily adapted to industrial needs; in one corner of a 14th-Century *wakalah* I found a one-man workshop, where a mechanic was busily welding the back axle of a truck.

It is easy to understand why hard-pressed occupants of an ever-more-crowded city should regard any building simply as potential room to live or work in, but the result of such lack of control has inevitably been the loss or deterioration of some of the many fascinating monuments of Cairo's past.

The physical decline of the Old City began in earnest about a century ago, when the wealthy merchant families who had dwelt there for centuries moved to the fashionable new European-style quarters of Cairo. They

In a poor quarter just south of the Old City, a line of washing unceremoniously drapes one of a row of the wooden bay windows, called mashrabiyahs, that characterized Cairo's domestic architecture in the 17th and 18th Centuries. Such lattice-work windows were designed to admit cooling breezes and light, while shielding the rooms within—especially the women's quarters—from outsiders' eyes.

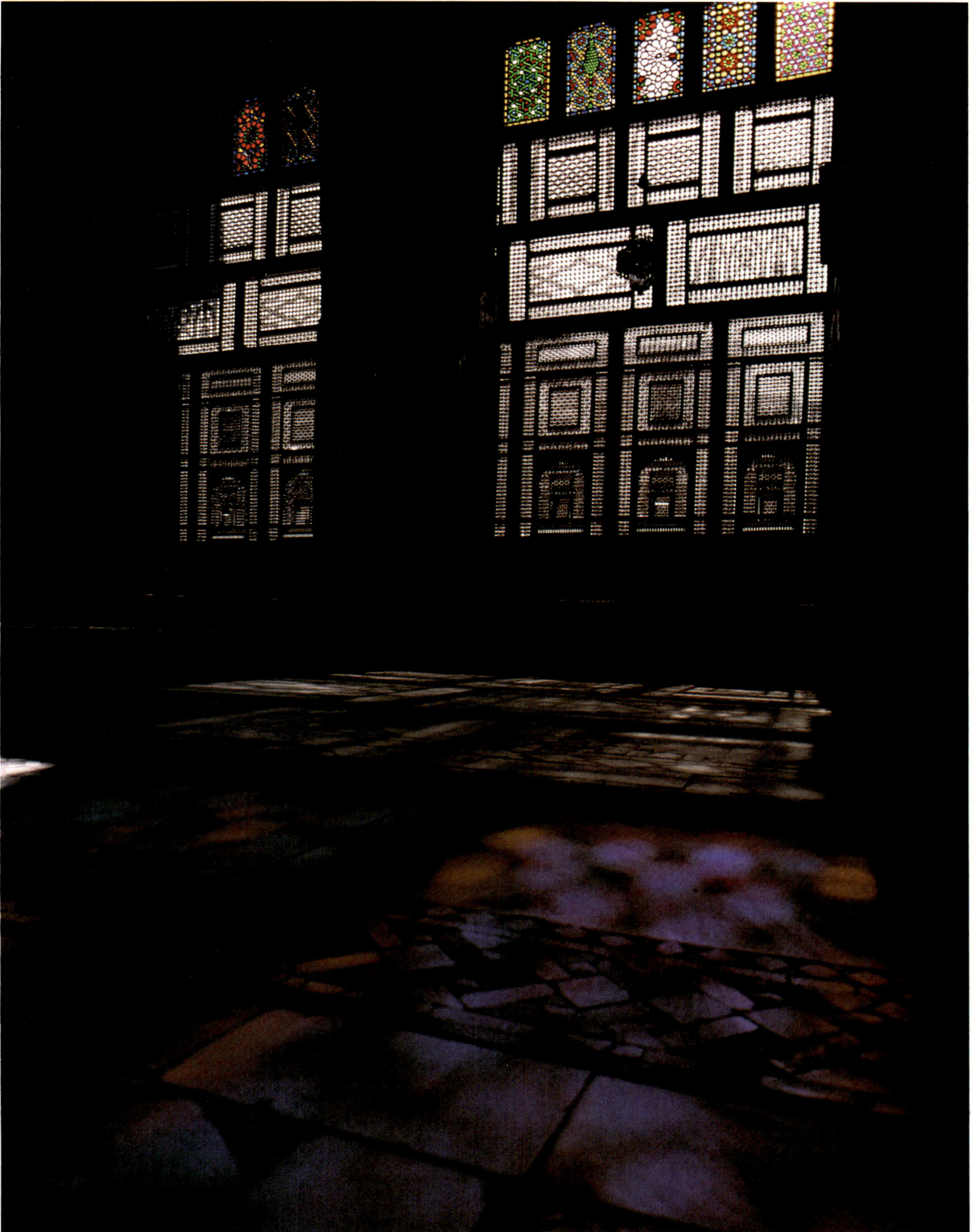

The lattice of a fine mashrabiyah, topped with stained-glass designs, filters sunlight into the Bayt al-Sihaymi, a restored 17th-Century house in the Old City.

were quickly followed by many of the local tradespeople. During the 1880s, in the face of the district's decline, a newly formed Committee for the Preservation of Monuments of Arab Art (a body composed almost entirely of European scholars) made an inventory of 622 buildings in Cairo thought worthy of preservation. This list, which was far from exhaustive, included mosques, palaces, colleges, convents, mausoleums, *wakalahs* and bath-houses dating from the 7th to the 19th Centuries, many of them unsurpassed examples of Islamic architecture. Today, more than a hundred of them have vanished.

Unlike most modern cities, medieval Cairo was never segregated into rich and poor areas. Each of the narrow *darbs* (alley-ways) that made up its labyrinth contained a cross-section of all levels of the city's society. The great family houses—whether lived in by a merchant, a lawyer or a master-craftsman—would have had a numerous complement of doormen, domestics and slaves. Attached to them might have been a *wakalah*, or perhaps a row of workshops for artisans and their apprentices. Across the way there was probably a *sabil-kuttab*, or "fountain school", where free drinking-water (downstairs) and free education (upstairs) were dispensed from the proceeds of a *waqf*—a pious endowment of land and property from a wealthy benefactor.

But a century ago foreign influences began to destroy this society; the élite moved out, abandoning the traditional texture of their life for Western chic. Once they had gone, only the poor were left; and they had neither the money nor the inclination to repair and improve the buildings. Since then, the side-effects of the Old City's desperate overcrowding have accelerated the decay. Fragile old structures of wood and brick stand little chance against the inexorably rising mountains of rubbish that the inhabitants pile against their walls, eventually causing them to collapse, or against leaking sewers that undermine their foundations. Even sturdy stone buildings are not proof against the looters of building material, or the innocent vandalism perpetrated by the neighbourhood's children.

The problem has been further exacerbated by the Islamic tradition of religious endowments. In the past, at least half of the Old City's public buildings, both sacred and secular, were erected and maintained by means of the income from some *waqf.* Over the centuries the yield from these endowments diminished; and, since 1952, they have been controlled by a government ministry that has with some justification given Cairo's grave social needs priority over the conservation of ancient buildings, spending the income instead on new housing developments and on mosques to serve the city's fast-growing outer suburbs. Responsibility for conservation now rests chiefly with the National Department of Antiquities, which, like every other public body in Egypt, is chronically short of cash. It has always devoted most of its limited funds to the restoration of pharaonic monuments, the country's chief tourist attractions and the main focus of Egypt's

Two Cairene women in country head-dresses pause to admire the jewellery in one of the many goldsmiths' shops clustered, for reasons of mutual security, in the heart of the medieval city's warren-like bazaar quarter. Gold is still favoured by many Cairenes as the safest form of investment and often makes up the bulk of a woman's dowry when she gets married.

interest in the past. Tourists seldom seem to venture into the chaos of the Old City to discover for themselves its magnificent heritage of Islamic architecture, and there is little official encouragement for them to do so. During my wanderings that day I saw scarcely a single other identifiable Westerner, save in the Khan al-Khalili.

But the will to save medieval Cairo certainly exists, at least at an official level, even if the money to do so is not yet forthcoming. There are plans to convert some of its gracious old caravanserais into hotels; Western governments have agreed to finance work on some of the ancient monuments—for example, the West Germans have recently restored the 14th-Century *madrasah* of Amir Mithqal in the northern part of the Old City. Foreign archaeological institutes would like to use the larger mansions as their headquarters—although the Egyptian authorities are said to be cautious about allowing them to do so, in case any future deterioration in international relations should, paradoxically, make these buildings the targets of anti-Western demonstrations.

In terms of striking the necessary balance between the conservation of the medieval city and the needs of its 20th-Century inhabitants, perhaps the most promising recent development was the setting up in 1977 of the Association for the Urban Development of Islamic Cairo, with the aim of counselling tenants on their legal rights, advising on harmonious designs for new buildings and establishing a political lobby to press for the protection of historic treasures. Meanwhile, the dilemma of the Old City is defined in the question: can a *modus vivendi* be found that will not sacrifice the people for the buildings nor the buildings for the people?

A Hand-Powered Economy

A worker moves between rows of mud-bricks, turning each one over to dry in the sun. The bricks will be used by the poor to build and repair their dwellings.

Prodigal of time and trouble, but scrupulously thrifty with its meagre natural resources, the pre-industrial sector of Cairo's economy provides a livelihood for about one quarter of the capital's labour force. In thousands of workshops all over the city, artisans—including metalsmiths and cabinet-makers, leather-workers and weavers—practise skills that have been passed on from generation to generation. Many activities are marked by a conspicuous ingenuity in the use and re-use of basic local materials—from Nile mud with which to mould bricks, to camel skins for making bags and wallets. The many workers who have no specialized skills are incorporated into the city's bottomless pool of labour ready to toil—as porters, vendors or labourers, for example—for minimal wages that make even the most labour-intensive methods economic.

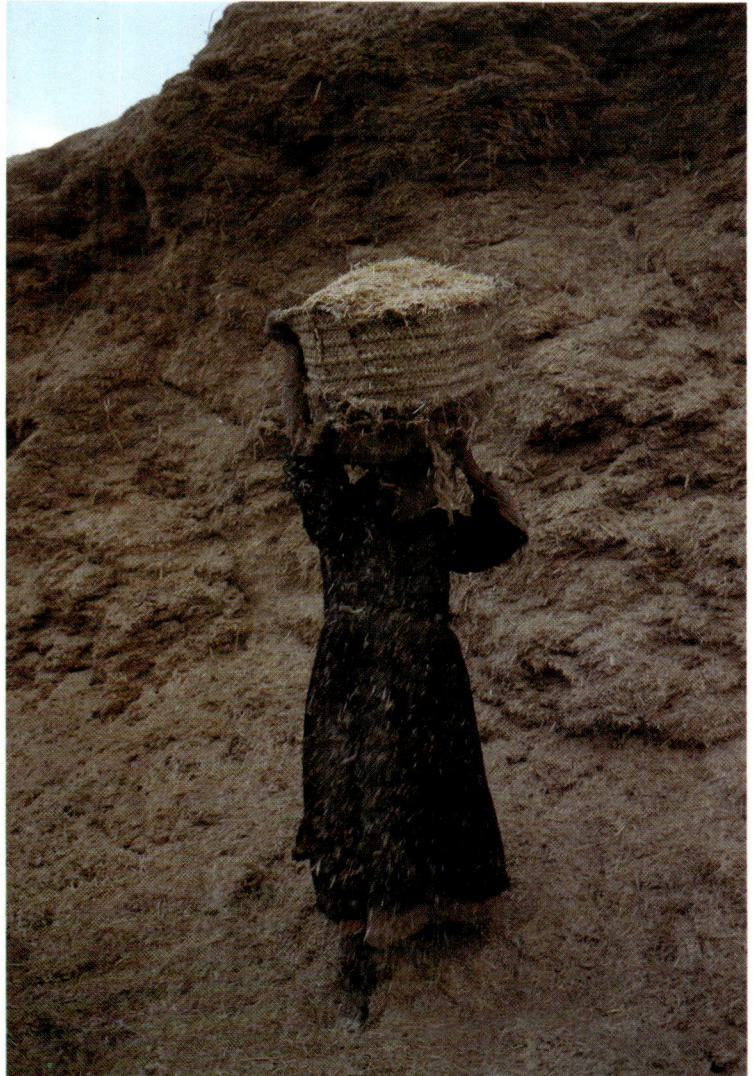

On the outskirts of Cairo, on the west bank of the Nile, peasants (left) sift out a second yield from the chaff remaining after the rice crop has been extracted by co-operatively hired machinery. Freed of dust and grit, the chaff is then borne away (above) to be used as bedding material for domestic animals.

To reduce waste, a young labourer carefully scrapes together dregs of cement.

Paid a pittance for their muscle-power, construction workers from Upper Egypt contribute to the modernization of Cairo's roads by carrying bags of cement.

To make atayif, the basis of a popular Egyptian sweetmeat, a cook carefully dribbles a flour and water paste on to a circular hotplate with an improvised ladle: a perforated coffee-pot. His tiny factory sells the cooked strands to housewives and commercial cake-makers in kilogram and half-kilogram bundles; when rolled up with honey, nuts and raisins, the atayif becomes kunafah—a sticky confection popular at religious festivals and holidays.

A craftsman weaves a durable rug with yarn made from waste scraps of fabric.

In an open-air workshop under a medieval aqueduct, dyed camel skins, tacked on wooden frames, are stretched to dry for use by the city's leather-workers.

Outside his workshop in the Old City's bazaar area, a metalworker embarks on a transitional stage for a large aluminium bowl. Two finished pieces lie nearby.

In a modern hotel's shopping complex for tourists, a coppersmith uses hammer and punch to imprint fine detail on a wall-plaque bearing a pharaonic design.

In one of Cairo's two remaining fez workshops a craftsman practises his trade. A piece of red felt is being formed into the familiar cylindrical shape on a mould that is kept hot by the brass oven below. A basketwork frame will then be glued underneath the cylinder. The red fez, or tarboosh, was introduced by the Ottoman Turks as a mark of official status, but is nowadays worn only by religious dignitaries.

3

Everyday Affirmations of Faith

If you climb up the Citadel on a summer evening, as the great orange disc of the sun begins to descend over the Pyramids, you will see a fantastic sight: the innumerable domes and minarets of Cairo outlined against a sky that turns turquoise before nightfall. The smooth, feminine contours of the domes seem to stabilize the soaring eccentricity of the minarets—octagonal, cylindrical or square towers that rise in tiers like wedding-cakes, some topped with miniature domes shaped like turbans, others with curving shapes that remind me of the funerary jars found in pharaonic tombs.

The majority of Cairo's minarets have balconies from which the muezzin (crier) summons the Muslim faithful to prayer. Five times daily, from mosques all over the city, the call to prayer—the *adhan*—rings out, as it has done for 13 centuries. It is a moving and beautiful sound, quite different from the church bells that fulfil the same function in Christian countries. The muezzins intone the *adhan* in their piercing, sonorous voices—somewhat nasal in timbre to Western ears—to a chant whose rhythm and melodic line are laid down by tradition; but each muezzin selects the pitch and tempo of his chant without reference to the others declaiming within earshot. The simultaneous but uncoordinated sounds remind me of modern choral compositions I have heard in which the composer discards conventional harmony to achieve a deliberate discord. Unfortunately, the effect of this gentle cacophony is nowadays marred by the widespread use of loudspeakers, that all too often suffer seizures and blur the balanced phrases of the call to prayer into a continuous and deafening, electronic hum.

Although Cairo numbers among its citizens communities of several religions and guarantees them absolute freedom of belief, none can challenge the supremacy of Islam. Some 90 per cent of Egypt's population are Muslims; Islam is the state religion; it is acknowledged by the Constitution and forms a strong bond between Egypt and other Islamic nations.

The only considerable minority group is that of the Coptic Christians, whose religion has come down to them in an unbroken tradition from the 1st Century A.D.—long before the advent of Islam—when Egypt had one of the earliest communities of Christian converts. About 10 per cent of Egyptians are Copts; but in Cairo itself, where about one fifth of the Copts live, the percentage is nearer 15. A very few Jews remain from the considerable community that existed in Cairo before the creation of the state of Israel in 1948, and their further general exodus following the Egyptian nationalist Revolution of 1952. Other communities—Protestant, Roman

In the courtyard of the mausoleum built by the medieval Sultan Barquq, an aged Cairene spends a quiet hour reading the Koran, the sacred book of Islam that many Muslims know by heart. The precepts of the Koran, revealed to the prophet Muhammad in the 7th Century, are still the chief authority guiding the lives of devout Muslims.

Catholic and Greek Orthodox Christians, for example—are small indeed, and are composed almost exclusively of foreign residents or the descendants of the city's European élite of pre-revolutionary days; they take no corporate part in Cairo's life.

Islam, however, is always and everywhere in evidence. It is far more than just a system of belief; it is a code of conduct that regulates every aspect of a Muslim's life. Forget that and you will never understand much that is puzzling in the day-to-day life of modern Cairo.

The word "Islam" means simply "submission"—that is, submission to the will of God. In practice, Muslims accept as the basis of their public and private life the teachings of the Koran, the book recording the holy doctrine which they believe was miraculously transmitted to the prophet Muhammad over a period of some 20 years, from A.D. 610 onwards. Muhammad did not consider himself the founder of a new religion, but rather the reformer of an old one: the monotheistic faith that is also embodied in the Old Testament books of the Bible. Muslims believe that Muhammad was "the seal of the prophets": the last and greatest in a long line of messengers sent by God to persuade mankind to return to the paths of righteousness. His predecessors included Abraham, Moses and Jesus, all of whom are held in especially high esteem in the Koran.

The revelations of the Koran—believed by the faithful to be the literal word of God—began on the "Night of Power", when Muhammad, an Arabian merchant then in his 40th year, was meditating in a cave at the foot of Mount Hira', near his home town of Mecca. He was visited by the Archangel Gabriel, who brought him the revelations and instructed him to "proclaim in the name of the Lord". And, obeying, Muhammad set about the task of evangelizing.

At first his preaching was fiercely resisted by the inhabitants of Mecca, whose prosperity depended largely on revenue from pilgrims to the city's popular pagan shrine. In 622, the year from which all Muslim dates are reckoned, Muhammad and his followers migrated to the city of Yathrib (later called, simply, al-Madinah—"the City"—implying the city of the Prophet) where Muhammad continued to preach. After defeating his opponents in battle, he succeeded in bringing Mecca under his control. The Bedouins of Arabia were rapidly converted and, by the time of his death in 632, Muhammad had become both the spiritual and temporal leader of the Arabs. He was followed as leader by a succession of his relatives, who bore the title of caliph. Within a century of the Prophet's death, the world of Islam stretched along a crescent from Spain to India.

The Koran is a work of literature unique in its vocabulary and form. There are short, ecstatic passages in wonderfully vivid language and detailed descriptions of the laws and duties regulating the daily life of Muslims, as well as longer, discursive accounts of the ancient prophets and the often terrifying fate of those who failed to heed them. During

Arms raised in exaltation, a white-clad woman bystander (above) breaks from the crowd to add her praise to the ecstatic procession of a Sufi brotherhood (right) during celebration of the prophet Muhammad's birthday. Sufism, a mystical movement within Islam, originated in the 10th Century and enjoyed a considerable revival in Cairo during the 1970s.

Muhammad's lifetime, so tradition states, the words of his revelations were not systematically written down, but recorded instead by the process of repetition and memorizing that is still an important part of Muslim observance today. In about the year 650 an authoritative written version of the revelations—the basis of the one existing today—was issued by the Caliph 'Uthman. In addition to the revelations, a collection of sayings and actions attributed to the Prophet, called the Hadith (Traditions), was compiled and committed to writing. Together, the Koran and the Hadith guide all Muslim religious and personal life.

The powerful prose of the Koran, with its combination of forceful rhetoric and rhythmic cadences, is superbly effective in oral delivery. The *qira'ah* (recitation of passages of the Koran) is beloved of Muslims, and its more skilled practitioners have always attracted an enthusiastic personal following. Wherever you go in present-day Cairo you are likely to hear the extraordinarily compelling voice of a *muqri'* (Koranic reciter) issuing from a transistor radio or from the cassette-players installed in many taxi-cabs.

Muslim tradition lays down, in prescribed order, five basic duties, or "Pillars of Faith": the profession of faith that "there is no god but God, and Muhammad is the messenger of God"; praying five times daily; giving alms (originally an obligatory contribution, now a private charitable duty); fasting daily throughout the month of Ramadan, the ninth month of the Muslim lunar calendar; and making at least one pilgrimage to Mecca during one's lifetime. Of these five duties, prayer is the most obvious outward sign of the presence of Islam in Cairo—as it is in every other Muslim community. At the appointed times—daybreak, noon, mid-afternoon, sunset and after nightfall—devout people will interrupt what they are doing, turn to face Mecca and bow down in prayer.

The ritual prayers at these times are most often repeated individually and privately, but communal prayer is also enjoined on Muslims in order to affirm their sense of community. The high point of the Muslim week is the special congregational prayer-service held every Friday—the Muslim holy day—at noon in the mosques. There are over a thousand mosques of every size in the city—quiet havens from the hectic bustle of the streets —ranging from small, private foundations to immense and often historic mosques where public services are held. The best-attended of all are those of al-Azhar and Sayyidna al-Husayn, east of the Old City's bazaars, and of Sayyidatna Zaynab, east of Garden City.

In these mosques, the long lines of worshippers follow the imam—the prayer leader—in the ritual sequence of actions, their rows of prayer-mats often overflowing into the streets outside and bringing the traffic to a respectful halt. The prayers vary somewhat from one time of day to another, but certain observances are universally obeyed. First, raising his hands on each side of his head, thumbs parallel to or even touching his ear-lobes, every worshipper utters the words "God is great", thereby symbolically cutting himself off at once from profane life and devoting himself to the worship of God. He then recites the first chapter of the Koran, al-Fatihah (the Opening). Next, he bows low while uttering the words "Glory be to my Lord most august." After straightening up, he kneels and touches his forehead to the ground, saying "Glory be to my Lord most high." He sits back on his heels and then prostrates himself once more in a demonstration of total submission to God. The complete sequence makes up a *rak'ah*, the basic unit of Muslim prayer.

Obligatory prayers consist of a minimum of two and a maximum of four *rak'ahs*. The worshipper concludes by sitting back on his heels to recite a prescribed liturgy, finally turning his head once to the right and once to the left as he says "Peace be upon you." These last words are popularly supposed to be addressed to angels attending him at each shoulder as he prays. At the Friday noon services, two of the usual *rak'ahs* are replaced by a sermon—occasionally in praise of official policy—followed by a moral exhortation. High-ranking members of the government and civil service make a point of attending these services.

There is no official priestly hierarchy in Sunni Islam. The imam is not an initiated intercessor between God and His worshippers and he has little formal authority. Although a learned imam will be respected for his erudition, his office is merely that of the poorly paid and easily replaceable administrator of the mosque in which he leads the prayers. Most imams have undergone some theological training before being employed, but small mosques with limited funds often have to content themselves with a relatively uneducated functionary. In Cairo, as in other Sunni communities, the real religious guidance resides chiefly with the body of professional teachers and theologians known collectively as the *'ulama'*— the informed or scholarly.

These masters of thought often have no official posts, but they are generally acknowledged to be the spokesmen of Islamic orthodox opinion. The authority of the *'ulama'* of Cairo extends to Sunni communities throughout the Islamic world; the reason is the continuing spiritual influence of the city's greatest religious institution, the mosque-cum-theological college of al-Azhar—the Resplendent. Founded by the Shi'ite Fatimids in A.D. 971 but converted to Sunni doctrines two centuries later by Saladin, al-Azhar is the world centre of Sunni Islam and perhaps the oldest functioning university in the world.

One afternoon, I found myself in the Old City near al-Azhar and took the opportunity to explore it. The rambling structure, whose five minarets are prominent Cairo landmarks, has experienced countless reconstructions and additions throughout the centuries; the chief surviving Fatimid part is the *sahn*, or inner courtyard, which is surrounded by an elegant colonnade of broad, pointed arches. There I saw a scene that cannot have changed

A Pattern of Piety

The group of letters that spell the word *Allah*—God—make a familiar motif that can be seen in the most varied contexts throughout Cairo, where nine tenths of the population are Muslim. The form of the word may vary slightly, according to the script employed; and it is often incorporated in a longer construction, such as that invoking God as "the Merciful, the Compassionate"; but the basic harmonious combination of vertical strokes and fluent lower curves always makes a pleasing flourish that is immediately recognizable, wherever it is seen.

The motif occurs frequently, of course, in mosques and on sacred articles; but since Muslims believe that God is omnipresent and that all events happen only by His will, nothing in the secular world is thought too humble to be inscribed with His name, whether as a simple but sincere demonstration of faith or a dedication of the object on which it appears.

1	2	3	4	5
6		7	8	9
10	11	12	13	14

 1 **As a decorative setting for calendars**
 2 **Above the prayer niche of a mosque**
 3 **A painted relief in a cobbler's shop**
 4 **On a chocolate good-luck charm**
 5 **In neon tracery on a snack-stall**
 6 **Furred with dust on an iron grille**
 7 **Garlanded on the door of a truck**
 8 **In concrete on a workshop wall**
 9 **Embossed in brass on a baker's oven**
10 **In fly-blown plaster outside a café**
11 **Embellishing a sidewalk foodstall**
12 **Built into a brick-kiln chimney**
13 **Written in lights for a festival**
14 **Adorning the front window of a truck**

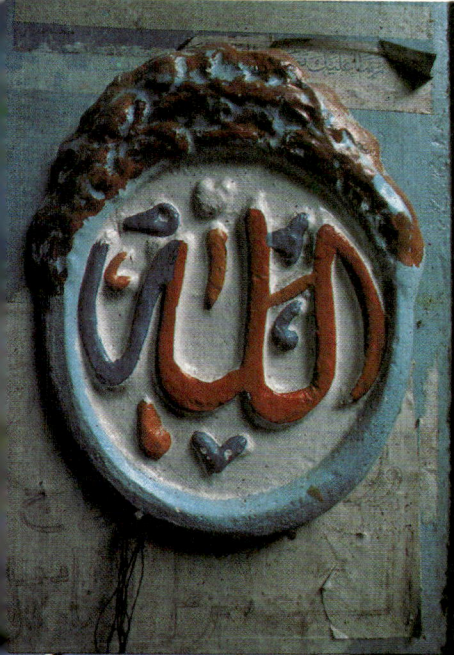
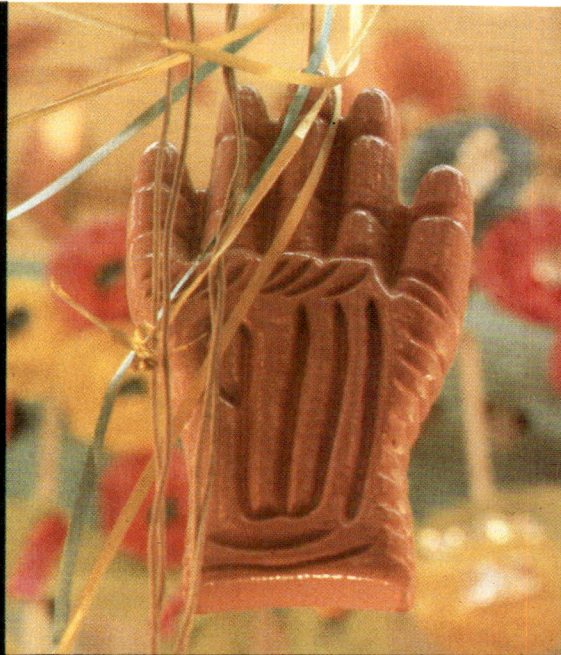

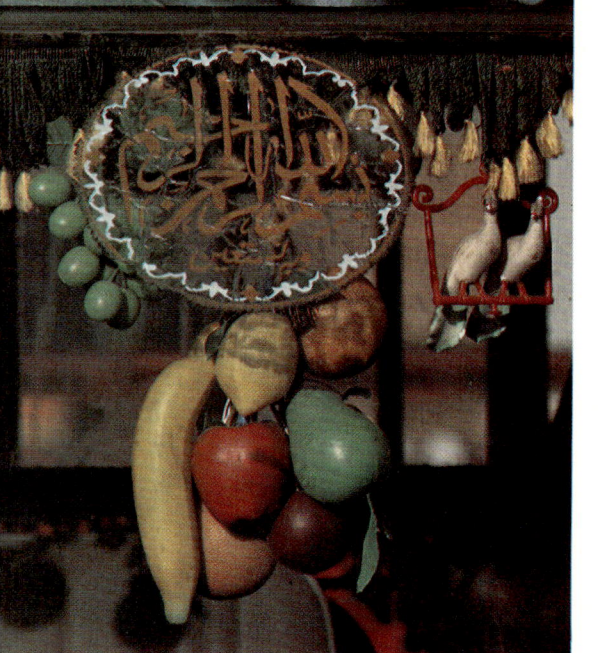

much in a thousand years. In the shade of the colonnade, groups of white-capped students sat on carpets around their tutors (members of the *'ulama'*), who were lecturing them on the twin pillars of traditional Islamic learning: the Koran and the Hadith. Other students strolled about, nodding and muttering as they memorized some commentary by a learned Koranic scholar of the past; perfect recall of the basic texts is still a requirement for anyone who aspires to erudition. Among those gathered I saw Javanese, black African and other non-Arab students. Al-Azhar still attracts scholars of every Muslim country, from Nigeria to Indonesia, and assigns to each national group a special portico and a common room for private study. These foreign students pay no tuition fees, and the poorer ones are provided with food and accommodation from pious bequests.

In the old days, students at al-Azhar were under no pressure to achieve specific grades or to pass examinations, since they were allowed a leisurely 15 years in which to complete their studies. Some of them were blind, attracted to the respected position of a religious teacher or a muezzin because of its emphasis on memory and oral skills; in the Middle East, where any infection is quickly aggravated by the flies and the dust, eye diseases have always been common. Today the courses in theology are more formally organized, leading to diplomas at various levels. There is still a tendency for blind students to gravitate towards religious life, for the same reasons as in the past.

The mosque of al-Azhar enjoys enormous prestige in the life of Cairo; during the Friday service, its courtyard is crowded with worshippers from all levels of the city's society. But the once-great political power of the *'ulama'* has waned considerably, especially during the 20th Century. The Sheikh or Rector of al-Azhar (sheikh is a word that means "elder", and is used as a title of respect for a learned man) used to have an authoritative voice in political affairs; in Islamic tradition there was no formal distinction between religious and secular authority, and so Islam, the State, society and the law were indissolubly linked. The legal and educational systems of Muslim countries, for example, were based directly upon Koranic teachings, and the law courts, schools and universities were staffed and administered by members of the *'ulama'*.

But increasing contact with Europeans throughout the 19th and 20th Centuries started a secularizing trend among Egyptian Islamic intellectuals, who aimed to modernize the country's institutions. They were resisted by strict traditionalists, who insisted that the revelations of the Koran were final and complete, and that any concessions towards Western thought and knowledge could only result in the dilution of Islam's perfection. In spite of efforts to find a flexible compromise between the extremes of traditionalism on the one hand and modernizing secularity on the other, the gap still exists between the adherents of each philosophy. The urban religious leadership and the unquestioningly pious humbler folk of both

Under the direction of their sheikh, or leader, the members of a Sufi brotherhood celebrating a Muslim festival engage in a ritual of chanting and swaying, designed to produce the hypnotic sense of union with God known as "dhikr", or remembrance. The many brotherhoods within Sufism each have their own formula of prayers and movements, first devised by the particular brotherhood's founder, that are performed at a variety of different religious occasions.

town and country are mainly traditionalists; the government leaders and the urban middle class increasingly tend to make a distinction between religious and secular spheres.

By the middle of the 20th Century, government and education had been largely secularized, and civil courts existed alongside the Islamic ones. In 1956 a decree of the government transferred the last powers of the religious courts to the civil system, a measure that severely curtailed the career prospects of the 'ulama' and hastened its transformation into a traditionalist enclave in a modernizing society.

But the process of secularization did not stop there. In 1961 al-Azhar itself was reduced to the level of a mere university, no different—in the eyes of the government—from the two other state universities in Cairo. Behind the medieval buildings where I saw the students studying the Koran, and on an outlying site in Nasr City near the suburb of Heliopolis, new campuses have been established to teach such technical subjects as medicine, commerce, agriculture and engineering—disciplines more relevant to Egypt's modern secular needs. In 1962 women were admitted for the first time; but as a gesture towards the traditionalists—including many of the students themselves—they occupy a separate department and have their own operating theatres in the medical school.

In present-day Egypt, continuing attempts are made to preserve the unity of political and religious interests. But where once the religious leaders took a controlling part in political matters, the converse now occurs: control of various religious matters has been assumed by the government. An official ministry takes responsibility for the maintenance of many of the mosques, and for the appointment and payment of officials in them, including imams and muezzins. By appointing well-educated men, the government tries to raise the educational standards of the congregations they preach to, and hence of the population as a whole.

In spite of certain tensions between government and religious authorities, the Sheikh of al-Azhar and other religious leaders—who are dependent on the government for funds—usually co-operate with government policies, sometimes expounding the Koran and other holy writings in support of official lines on—for instance—birth control or labour reform. In return, the civil authorities acknowledge and respect the faith and its leaders. The Constitution adopted in 1971 reaffirmed Islam as the official religion of Egypt, and government speeches and documents nowadays frequently make reference to Muslim terms, laws and customs, while religious duties and ceremonial rites are punctiliously and publicly observed by individual politicians.

Nevertheless, conflict does arise. Fundamentalist groups who resist—sometimes with violence—the government's tendency towards secularity and Western modernism often consider the 'ulama' to be part of the establishment they attack. In Egypt, a country with a 60 per cent illiteracy rate, the spoken word still has the power to move people, and the spirit of political protest sometimes finds expression in traditional oral forms. The work of a controversial blind singer, Sheikh Imam 'Isa, is a case in point. The son of a poor glass-maker from Gizah, Imam 'Isa was brought up with an ultra-conservative Muslim sect (which eventually expelled him for listening to a *muqri'* on that unacceptable foreign innovation, the radio) and later studied singing, recitation, composition and lute-playing with leading teachers of Arab classical music. During the 1960s Imam 'Isa's satirical songs about contemporary political abuses won him an immense popular following among the students and young people of Egypt. He turned down lucrative offers to work with the government television and radio network, preferring instead to give impromptu recitals to gatherings of students and friends.

One evening in Cairo several years ago, during the month of Ramadan, I attended a private performance he gave at the house of friends. Imam 'Isa, a frail-looking man in dark glasses, seemed much older than his 50 years, but as soon as he began to sing, tapping out a rousing rhythm on the sound-board of his lute, a fierce energy animated his face. With the nasal, plaintive delivery of Koranic recitation, but using the vigorous vocabulary of the Cairo streets, he sang ditties that satirically rebuked the authorities for mismanaging the country and using religion as a cloak to cover their misdeeds. The audience joined in the refrain.

The Sheikh had suffered some harassment at the hands of the authorities. When I visited him, he had only recently been released from prison where he had been summarily detained along with other critics of the

Flanked by fellow dignitaries, the Rector of the great Muslim university of al-Azhar waits to receive guests in one of the many magnificent tents set up throughout the city for annual ceremonies that mark the Prophet's birthday. Such tents, enclosing a space on three sides only, feature richly appliquéd hangings; they serve as settings for many high occasions, from religious festivals to weddings or funerals.

regime. He therefore stopped short of openly inflammatory utterances. As a conclusion, he contented himself with an ode to peace:

> *Peace is a green word*
> *Like the tender branches of sweet basil*
> *That moistens the lips*
> *When it swims on the tongue.*

In spite of the increasing government intervention in the management of religious affairs, and the secularizing outlook of many of Cairo's middle class, it would be a mistake to conclude that Islam had receded from the lives of most of the people. Its formal aspects may indeed have lost some ground since the Revolution, but I was much impressed by the pervasive influence of popular and unorthodox forms of Islam among the largely illiterate and uneducated mass of the people. Such unquestioning belief has always been characteristic of country people and, with the great influx of fellahin into the city in recent decades, the popular religion has come to take on a new and growing importance in the capital too.

The devout feelings of the people are made manifest in various ways: in the modest dress and beige headscarves of a traditionalist movement called the Muslim Sisters; in a general reluctance to take the values of Western society on trust; and most particularly in the processions, gatherings and ecstatic trances that are associated with the popular religious phenomenon known as Sufism.

The great wave of Sufism first spread over the Muslim world a thousand years ago, at least three centuries before the wandering friars of St. Francis and St. Dominic in Europe were preaching voluntary poverty and the simple life. Like the Christian reformers, the first Sufi leaders (so-called because they wore a plain undyed garment made of wool—*suf*) wished to escape from the pomp and worldliness that had overtaken their religion and return to the simplicity of the original faith.

The movement reached its height in the 17th and 18th Centuries, when the majority of Muslim males in Cairo belonged to one of the hundreds of brotherhoods. With the passage of time the brotherhoods, often criticized as backward-looking and superstitious, shrank in numbers and importance; but in the 1970s there were signs of a considerable revival.

The activities of each brotherhood are focused upon reverence for a particular sheikh or holy man, who in his lifetime has earned the title of *wali*—a kind of local saint. The word *wali* means "friend" or "companion", for the *walis* are considered to have attained by their holiness a close companionship with God. There is nothing in the Koran to justify the cult of the *walis*; but with the renewed popularity of the brotherhoods, it is practised widely throughout Cairo.

Each saint has his own reverenced tomb, sometimes a mosque dedicated to him and—above all—his own *mulid* or birthday celebration. The

Mementoes of Mecca

The *hajj*, or pilgrimage to Mecca—a solemn duty that the Koran enjoins all Muslims to perform at least once in their lifetime—is an event so momentous that the pilgrim's family customarily proclaims his piety by adorning the outside of his house with drawings recording the journey to Mecca, the holy places in and near the sacred city, or the rituals that are required of the pilgrims.

Instead of making their way by the overland caravans of the past, today's pilgrims—as the wall-paintings of Cairo make clear—move by the most modern forms of transport. However, although the means of travel have changed, the essential rituals of the *hajj* have barely altered in 13 centuries. On arrival in the holy city, every pilgrim makes his way to the courtyard of the Sacred Mosque to approach the Ka'abah, a black-draped, cube-shaped shrine originally built —according to Muslim tradition—by Abraham himself, who is revered by Muslims, Jews and Christians alike as the first prophet of their monotheistic faith.

The rituals performed by the pilgrims during their 10-day sojourn include a visit to the desert valley of Mina, where they throw pebbles at three pillars symbolizing the Devil.

There also each pilgrim slaughters an animal to commemorate the devotion of Abraham, who in that same valley was even prepared to sacrifice his own son at God's command—an act of faith that the Almighty rewarded by sending an angel with a ram to be sacrificed instead.

Images of a camel caravan and an airliner share a housefront with the words "Blessings on the Prophet".

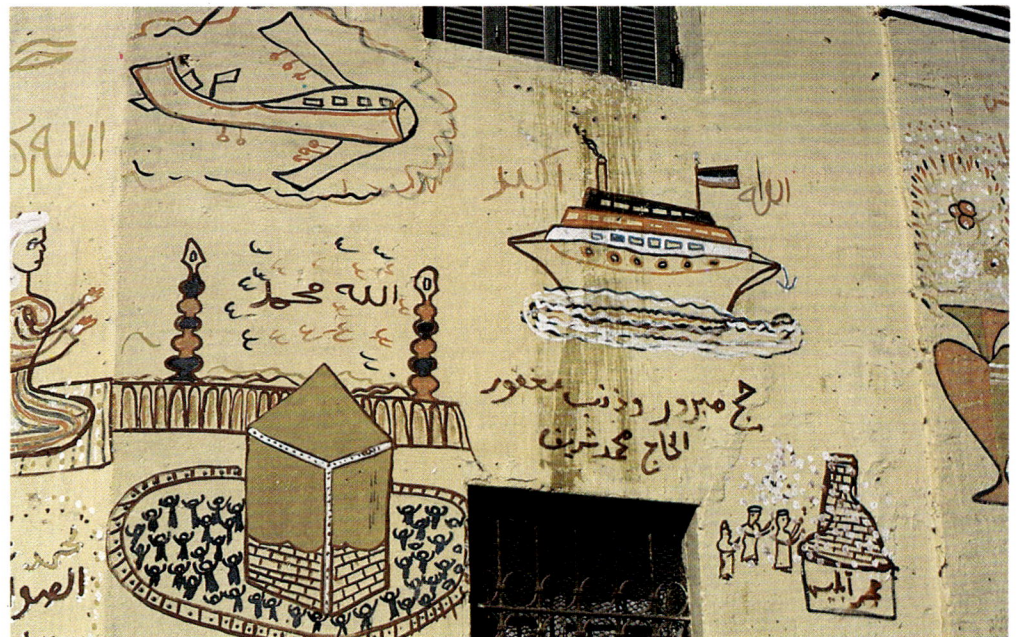

This mural includes a representation of the Ka'abah at Mecca and the ritual stone-throwing at Mina.

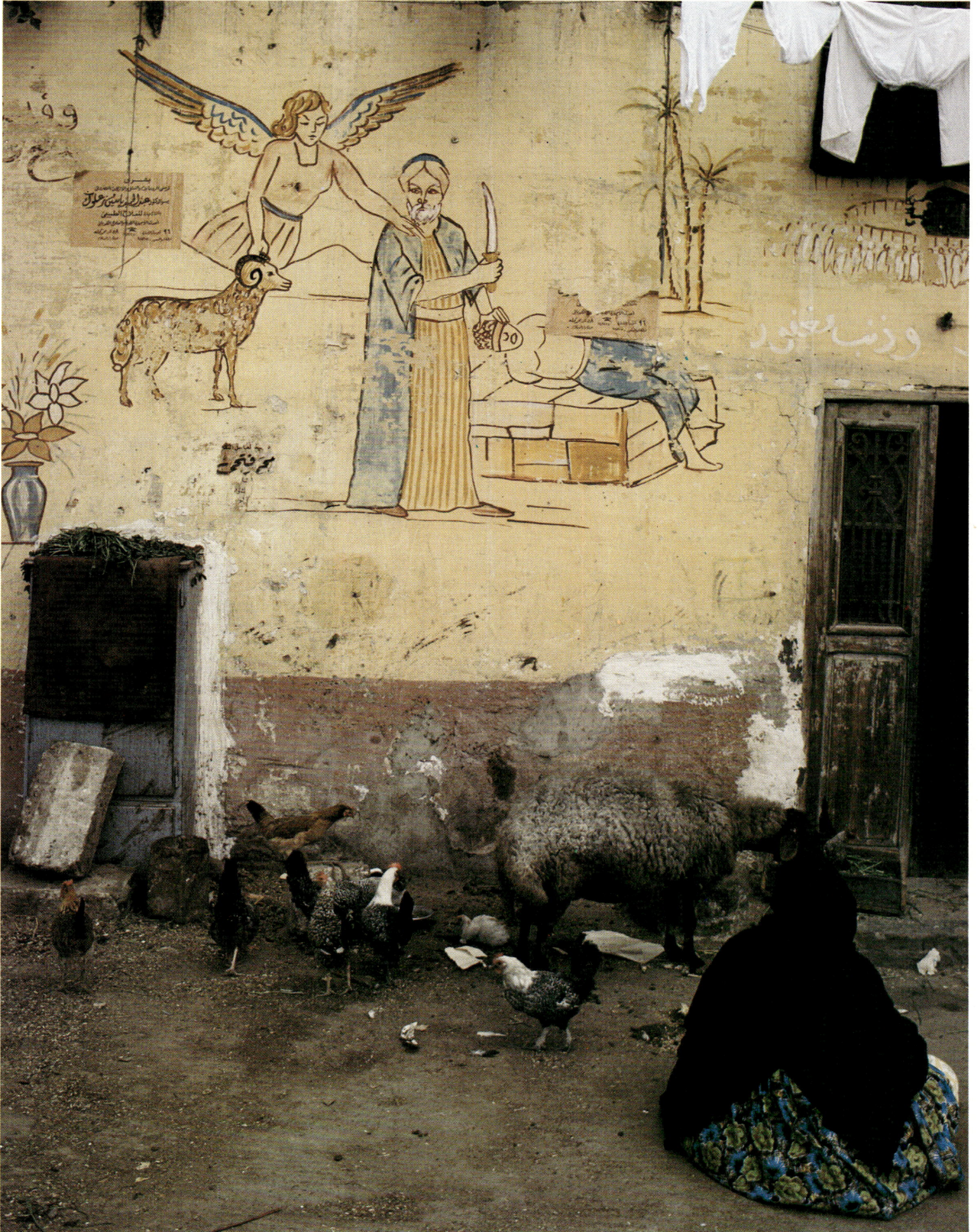

A carefully drawn scene on the courtyard wall of a pilgrim's house recreates the biblical story of the angel who prevents Abraham from sacrificing his son.

A broad avenue in one of the city's immense and ancient cemeteries is flanked by stately entrances to tombs built around an inner courtyard, on the age-old pattern of living quarters built for the Arab affluent. These unique Cities of the Dead on Cairo's eastern border contain some medieval tombs of great architectural beauty; but many—including those shown—are family tombs erected as recently as the 19th and 20th Centuries.

saint's *mulid* constitutes one of the big events of the year for the members of a brotherhood and their families. Thousands may gather to participate in the celebrations, which are centred upon the tomb or mosque, and last a designated number of days—from three or four to 14 or so. Swings and roundabouts are erected in the surrounding streets, stalls selling drinks and sweetmeats appear, and ceremonial tents are raised to serve as temporary headquarters for the brotherhood. The tents are ornate hangings appliquéd with striking arabesque designs in red, gold and green. With their dirt floors carpeted, and furnished with gilt chairs and inlaid tables, the tents can be seen all the year round throughout Cairo, providing a festive setting not only during *mulid* celebrations, but also for wedding receptions and many other ceremonies. The tents are made in the Street of the Tent-Makers just south of the Old City; and there are evidently enough special occasions to keep the tent-makers busy.

At the *mulids*, an atmosphere of intense excitement and near-hysteria is aroused by the characteristic ritual of the *dhikr*. The word *dhikr* means "remembrance" or "bringing to mind"; and the rituals—employed at all sorts of occasions, from weddings to funerals—usually rely on the chanting of a formula or an incantation made up of the many names of God combined with a variety of prayers. They are designed to put the celebrants into an ecstatic, trance-like state of mind in which they feel at one with God. The chants may be accompanied by a repeated series of vigorous physical movements that enhance their hypnotic effect. Many brotherhoods have their own particular *dhikr* formula, handed down to them by their *wali*.

The climax of the *mulid* comes on the last day, when a ceremonial procession approaches the saint's tomb—considered to be extremely holy, since in popular belief the soul of the *wali* still lingers there. The members of the brotherhood press closely around the tomb and touch it in the hopes of transferring to themselves its *barakah*—the spiritual virtue or blessing that they believe resides there.

Inspiration for the development of such brotherhoods is unpredictable, and succession to the leadership is not governed by any formal rules. Some brotherhoods flourish for centuries, but some wither away again after their charismatic founder disappears. The *walis* upon whom the brotherhoods concentrate their belief and devotion may belong to any period of history, from the earliest to the most recent. Two of the most popular of Cairene saints are the Prophet's granddaughter, Sayyidatna ("Our Lady") Zaynab, and his grandson, Sayyidna ("Our Lord") al-Husayn, who was killed in A.D. 680 after challenging the authority of the caliphs of Damascus; both have important mosques dedicated to them. At the other end of the scale, Sheikh Salamah, the *wali* of one of the most popular of today's brotherhoods, died as recently as 1939.

Sheikh Salamah was a minor civil servant, a clerk in the Lands Department under the British administration before the Second World War. His

photograph is perhaps the most precious possession of his followers, who carry it with them at all times and recount, again and again, the folklore that has already grown up around his beloved figure: stories of his generous nature, of his skill as a teacher and expounder of the Hadith (for, though uneducated in religious controversy, he could, it is claimed, confound the *'ulama'*, much as Jesus confounded the Pharisees), and of his devotion to the name of God, which he is credited with having recited 30,000 times each night for six years—only one example of the many miracles that the Sheikh is said to have performed during his lifetime.

The members of the brotherhood (named the Hamidiyah Shadhiliyah after two earlier Sufi sheikhs) gather every year in the district of Bulaq to celebrate Sheikh Salamah's *mulid*, which grows more splendid with every passing year. When I witnessed it in 1978, thousands of the faithful had streamed into Bulaq for the four-day festival from neighbouring quarters of the city and even from surrounding country villages.

Each local branch of the brotherhood had pitched its own ceremonial tent on the patch of open ground that surrounded the shrine and mosque of Sheikh Salamah, and throughout the festivities each vied with the others in the simple splendours of the hospitality they gave; tea and sweetmeats were handed round, singers and instrumentalists provided musical entertainment. The occasion had the joyous atmosphere of a family holiday; for, although wives and daughters were not permitted to enter the tents while their menfolk were taking part in the *dhikr* ceremonies, they swarmed around outside in an excited, chattering throng.

After dark on the last day of the *mulid*, the climax approached. Through the neon-lit ceremonial arches hung with portraits of President Sadat that had been erected in the surrounding streets, a solemn procession arrived, headed by the brotherhood's present leader, Ibrahim, son of the *wali*. *"Ya Sidi Salamah! Ya Sidi Ibrahim!"* cried the crowds, calling on the names of the *wali* and his son, as they surged forward to touch the hem of their leader's robe, in the hopes of acquiring *barakah*.

Any visitor to Cairo should make a point of arriving during one of its major festivals: the *mulid* of Sayyidna al-Husayn (which lasts for 15 days and 14 nights); of the Prophet himself; of Sayyidatna Zaynab; or perhaps the feast of 'Ashura', the anniversary of Husayn's martyrdom, which is celebrated on the 10th day of Muharram, first month of the Muslim year. Unfortunately, it is impossible to give precise dates; the Muslim calendar follows the lunar year, so that each festival, being dependent upon the waxing and waning of the moon, occurs approximately 10 days earlier in each successive year. This endless shifting of dates is an enormous source of confusion to foreign visitors and to the government tourist board alike. Ironically, the only feasts that occurred unchangingly at the same season of the year were those erstwhile celebrations associated with the

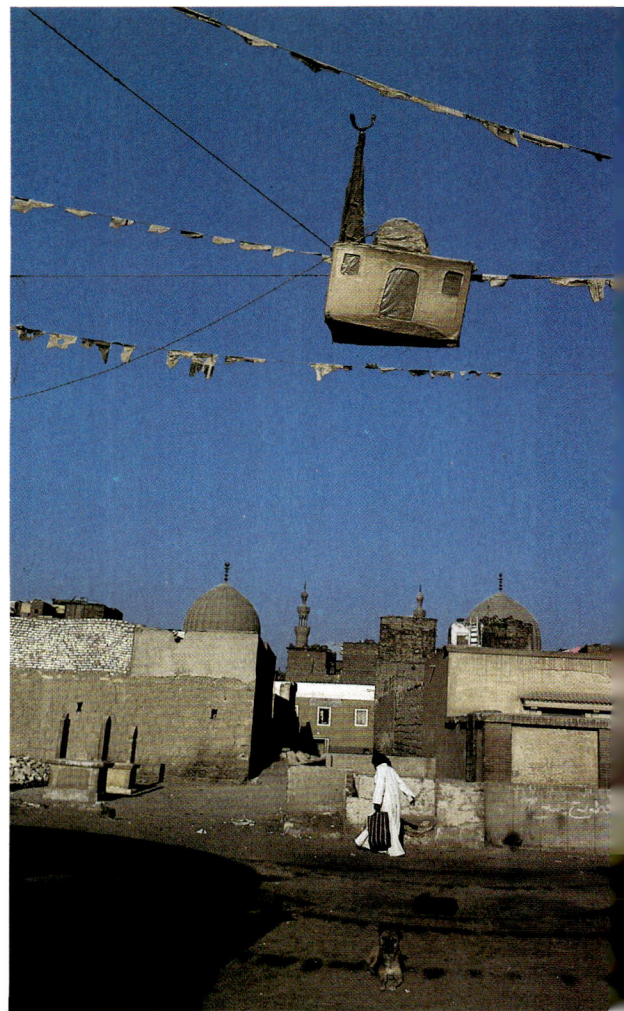

Rigged up by some of the squatters who have made their homes in the house-like tombs of Cairo's Cities of the Dead, paper streamers and a flimsy cardboard "mosque" are suspended high over the Northern Cemetery (above) in celebration of a Muslim festival. In a cemetery courtyard (right), two women do their washing. In spite of the absence of such basic municipal services as water and drainage, some areas of the cemeteries have well-established communities with their own shops and cafés.

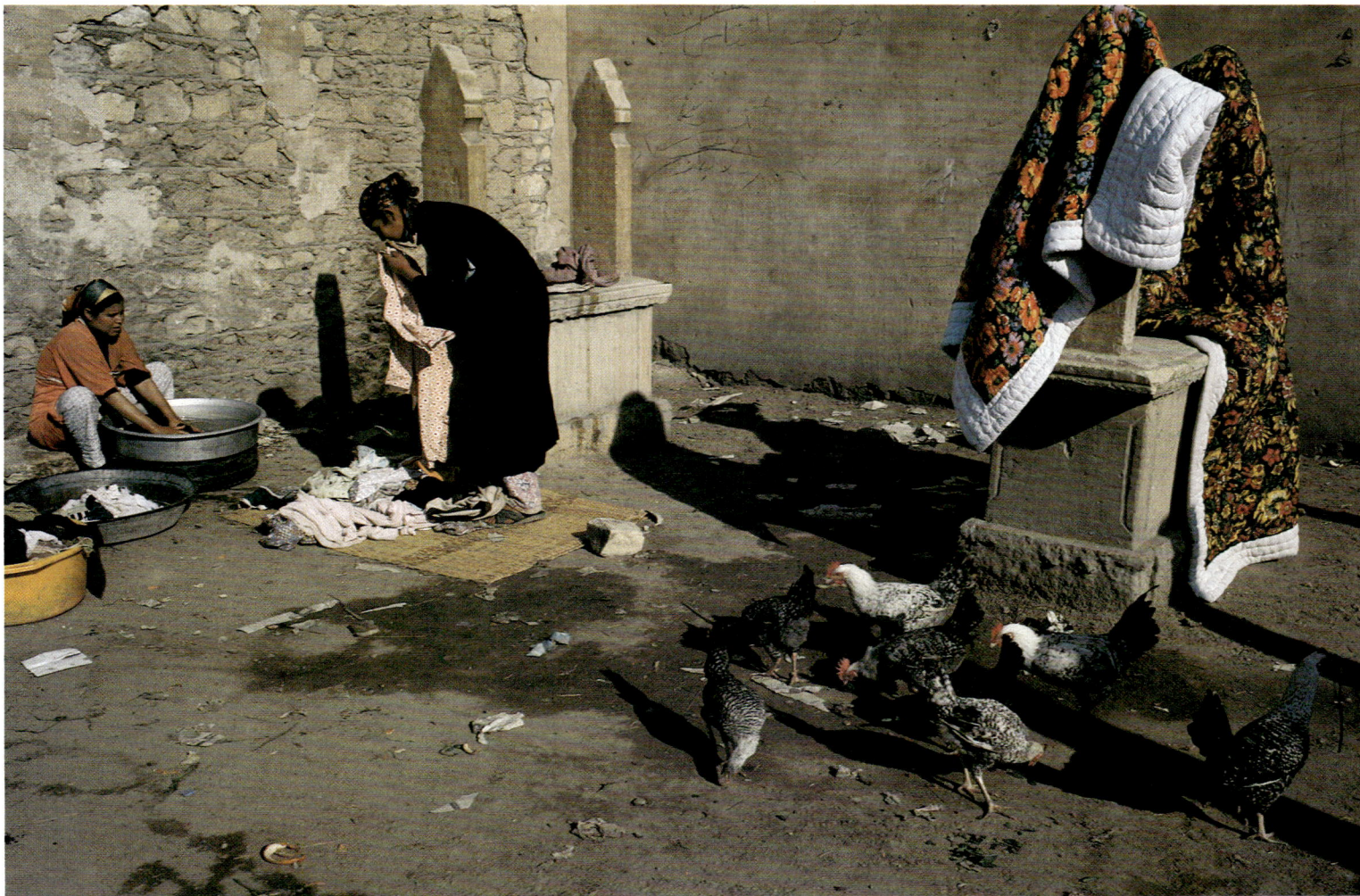

annual flooding of the Nile; but with the artificial regulation of the river's level, they have become little more than a fond memory.

The cycles of the lunar calendar cause no confusion, however, to the citizens of Cairo, for whom the great festivals follow each other in an unchanging and unchallengeable sequence known to all. Of all the events in the Cairo year, the longest-lasting and most widely observed is that of Ramadan, the ninth month of the Muslim year, during which God's revelations first came to Muhammad. For the whole month, all Muslims observe the fourth precept of the "Pillars of Faith" and fast from dawn to sunset.

The hours of fasting begin when it becomes possible to distinguish a thread of dawn light in the blackness of the night sky, and end when the sun's disc sinks below the horizon. During this period the faithful should abstain not only from eating and drinking, but also from sexual intercourse and smoking. At Cairo's latitude, when Ramadan falls in mid-winter, daylight lasts a mere 12 hours, but when the Holy Month falls in the height of summer, an almost unbearable 16 hours of abstention are demanded at the hottest time of the year. It is not too onerous to go without food for a day; I have often done this unintentionally in Cairo's scorching summers, which take away the appetite. But to abstain as well from all liquids, especially the frequent cups of tea and coffee on which people rely to keep themselves going in the heat, is truly arduous.

The sacrifice is all the harder for Cairenes; unlike Muhammad's austere warriors, accustomed to the hardships of desert life, they are a sensuous and pleasure-loving people. They therefore make Ramadan endurable by convincing themselves that abstinence increases the pleasure to come. The chain-smoker can get through the day by contemplating the ecstasy of that first puff after sundown, the hungry gourmet by the thought of a delicious meal at dusk. Even in the poorest homes the women devote great effort to preparing this evening meal, the *iftar*, determinedly ignoring government appeals to reduce the quantity of flour used in making *ka'k*, the short-pastry cookies peculiar to Ramadan. The shortages of certain foods that arise periodically in Egypt—usually caused by the diversion of hard currency to other sectors of the economy—seem never to happen during Ramadan; even the butchers, normally limited to selling meat four days a week, are permitted to trade every day.

Days and nights are turned inside out during Ramadan. In daytime the city moves with a dreary lassitude. People arrive late for work and leave early, taking prolonged siestas to see them through the afternoon. Many haunt the mosques, where the general drowsiness is clearly in evidence. One day, when I abandoned my own siesta and wandered into al-Azhar during the afternoon sermon, I found most of the occupants asleep—not, as in Western churches, gently nodding in the pews, but fully stretched out under the columns, like hunters resting in a forest. When the time for prayer came around, they wakened and prayed.

Of course, the people of Cairo vary in the strictness of their observance of Ramadan. The less devout defer to public opinion by refraining from eating or smoking in public; but in the privacy of a home or office it is not unusual to be served tea or coffee, or to be invited by friends to share a meal, as at other times of the year. The city's poor tend to take the Holy Month more seriously and, since they provide the sinews of the city, the lethargy of Ramadan ultimately affects everyone. Servants reduce their movements to a waif-like shuffle. Drivers let their vehicles wander aimlessly from one side of the street to the other, collisions become more frequent and tempers increasingly frayed.

At last, mercifully, sunset comes. A cannon booms from the Citadel, as it does every night of Ramadan—the city's dinner gong. The morose, seemingly interminable daylight hours are over. The fuming traffic miraculously vanishes and the city falls silent, except for the subdued murmurs of voices in the cafés and the tinkling of glassware. The main streets are deserted as people return home to devour their *iftar*. During this magic hour one can walk through all of Cairo without being jostled by the usual omnipresent crowd.

However, it is not long before people and traffic begin to flood back on to the streets. Although the thoroughfares are soon clogged and the din becomes appalling as drivers vent their frustration by leaning on their horns, the sudden gaiety is extraordinarily stimulating. The people, dull and unsmiling during the day, become lively and friendly. They greet you in the street, inviting you to tea or coffee. They chain-smoke. The sudden infusion of stimulants into the body's starved system often has an electrifying effect. I shall never forget an evening taxi ride from Gizah to Ma'adi with a driver, just come from his *iftar*, who hurtled blithely down the road oblivious of children, animals, a donkey cart, three other cars and an oncoming bus. On a personal social level, of course, the effect is more agreeable—although, as one's neighbours often sit up all night chatting, listening to Koranic recitations on the radio, or waiting for the meal before sunrise, sleep comes hard even to the weary infidel.

Intended to be a month of austerity and restraint, Ramadan has been converted by the natural Egyptian instinct for celebration into a period of self-indulgence; the food import bill doubles and people actually eat twice as much as in any other month. But even so, as Ramadan draws to a close, the high spirits of the night become a little jaded and Cairenes seem relieved that the end is in sight.

Shortly before the end comes, however, there is one special vigil to be kept—at least by the devout, who flock to the mosques to pray throughout the hours of darkness. The occasion is the anniversary of the Night of Power itself, the 27th night of Ramadan. At this time, angels are believed to descend between dusk and dawn to confer blessings upon the poor; the gates of heaven are open and prayers are therefore certain of success. Anyone who is born or who dies during this auspicious night is popularly considered to be especially blessed.

Two or three days later, the cannon fires for the last time. Just as Ramadan begins—with the sighting of the hairbreadth crescent of the new moon (and the evidence of one Muslim witness is sufficient for the proclamation of the fast)—so it ends when the succeeding new moon rises and is observed. A wave of collective relief, almost tangible in its intensity, surges over the city. The fast is over.

Soon after sunrise on the first day of the new month, houses and apartments all over Cairo are crowded with families and their friends. They embrace and congratulate each other, delighted that they can again eat and drink and smoke in the normal way. Once more the crowds and the traffic surge into the streets, the children turned out for the occasion in bright new clothes. The air crackles with the sound of fire-crackers that young boys ignite in the roads or on the pavements and under the skirts of passers-by. This is the day-long 'Id al-Fitr, the Feast of the Breaking of the Fast. After the initial high spirits have worn off, Cairo changes its mood once more, and most of the inhabitants, remembering their ancestors, take a new direction—to the Cities of the Dead.

Cairo's great cemetery areas run north and south of the Citadel, and cover almost two square miles. Originally on the eastern outskirts of the city, the broad expanse occupied by the Cities of the Dead marked, since the early days of its existence, the limit of Cairo's eastward expansion, until the advent of modern building methods made it possible to colonize the Muqattam Hills beyond.

These are no ordinary cemeteries with simple tombstones and ceno-taphs, such as can be found in most Islamic countries, but real necropolises, with well-regimented streets and rows of solidly built stone houses in domestic style, often with resident caretakers, known as *bawabs* (door-men). The tombs are family properties and are modelled on private dwellings, with an open courtyard and adjoining rooms. The vaults are usually built under the courtyard and the steps leading down to them filled in with stones and rubble, to be unearthed for each subsequent burial. The vaults contain separate chambers for men and women, so that the sexual segregation fundamental to the Islamic way of life can be maintained even in death.

These tombs are often in better condition, and better furnished, than the flats and houses of the family's living members. I have a friend who says that the quality of the silverware in his family mausoleum is far superior to anything in the fine old mansion where he still lives; many of the family's valuables had to be sold in the lean years after the 1952 Revolution, whereas those locked up in the vault of the mausoleum were, of course, sacrosanct. Some families do let their tombs fall into disrepair or, if their fortunes decline, even sell them to others who have "arrived" socially or financially; but, generally speaking, the devotion with which Egyptians observe their duties to the dead is remarkable. One has only to compare the rubbish-strewn streets and crumbling houses of the Old City with the well-ordered neatness of parts of the Eastern Cemetery to perceive the important role death still plays in the attitudes of Egyptians.

In recent years large areas of the Cities of the Dead have been occupied and urbanized by squatters. There has, of course, always been a sizeable population of *bawabs* and their families who made their permanent homes in the tomb-houses. But as Cairo's population has been increasing, many of them have been joined by relatives and friends; and other urban immigrants have occupied tombs that were abandoned. Thus, a living city with an estimated half million inhabitants has grown up in the Cities of the Dead, with grocery stores, cafés and markets. Even now, though certain of these cemetery areas are becoming overcrowded, the quality of the housing available there is generally superior to that in other parts of Cairo, since the tombs are commodious and structurally sound. There is nothing macabre or lugubrious about such places. No one seems to care that there are a few dozen bones buried under the living-room floor, and a marble cenotaph can make a convenient surface on which to slice onions or to perch an oil stove.

Visits to the Cities of the Dead by families of the deceased are usually made on the anniversary of a relative's death; but there are also certain dates when a general visitation to the cemeteries takes place, and even

Her hands stained crimson by the cochineal dye used to colour icing sugar, a young girl (above) decorates a paper sail that will complete the making of a moulded sugar boat—one of the elaborate confections sold at Cairo's sweet-stalls during major religious festivals. On their way to market, a trayful of decorated sugar dolls called "arusahs" (brides) is borne aloft (right) by a cheerful delivery-man.

families who have no particular tomb to visit often participate. The chief of these occasions occurs on 'Id al-Fitr at the end of Ramadan and on 'Id al-Adha' (Feast of the Sacrifices), the 10th day of the 12th month of the Muslim calendar; but they also take place several other times a year, on the major religious feast-days.

The families arrive in the manner appropriate to their social status: the rich, in luxury automobiles; the poor, in horse-drawn carts or on foot; the people in between, in battered taxis. Each group makes for its family tomb and, before long, the streets are alive with the murmur of picnickers and the blare of cassette-recorders playing qira'ahs. The families bring with them *fitir rahmah* (meaning "meal of mercy")—a picnic of everyday food, including perhaps watermelon and other fruit, beans and the chick-pea balls called *ta'miyyah*. Food and money are donated to the poor: usually accompanying friends or relatives, but also other needy people who happen to be nearby. After the meal, the families sit around in the court-yards listening to a Koranic reciter whom they may have hired to deliver a memorial *qira'ah*, or simply chatting.

The morning of a feast-day is, of course, a particularly good time to visit the cemeteries; one can then look inside tombs that are normally closed. Apart from the few surviving medieval mausoleums—some of which (for example, that of the 15th-Century Mamluk Sultan, Qa'it Bay) are among the most beautiful examples of Islamic architecture in existence —the majority of the tombs are of recent origin, dating from the 19th and 20th Centuries. Their appearance is nevertheless mostly traditional, incorporating Mamluk-style domes in stone or cement, doorways dripping with "stalactite" decoration, or walls topped with elaborate crenellations. But the more innovative builders have produced some surprises. Looking into a fairly new tomb from which a visiting family had just departed, I found that it resembled a 1930s Hollywood film set: a tiled courtyard with a loggia of round, stucco arches, in the best art deco style.

In spite of the physical existence of the Cities of the Dead, orthodox Muslim tradition has no place for a cult of the dead. It forbids embalming or burning of the corpse, and requires immediate burial with a minimum of fuss. Once again, as with many Islamic practices in Egypt, the letter of the law is observed but the spirit is quite another matter. True, the body of the deceased is disposed of, if practicable, by sundown on the day of death. But while in most Muslim countries that is considered to be the end of the affair, in Egypt it is only the beginning. The rites of consolation, where the bereaved receive the condolences of friends and relatives, are sometimes held in as many as three places for the same individual: his home village, the house where he died (in which the women of his family mourn), and, for male mourners, one of those beautiful appliquéd tents that populate the city. These receptions—at which the mourners sit on gilt chairs drinking coffee, listening to a *muqri'* and expressing and receiving condolences—take place on three successive Thursday evenings after the death, on the 40th day and on subsequent anniversaries. Naturally, the expense of such obsequies is considerable and the funerals of some poorer people are financed from charitable endowments or by co-operative associations that exist solely for this purpose.

Although there can be no doubt that Cairo is essentially an Islamic city, it is nonetheless not exclusively Islamic. While in the Old City and in many of the new suburbs there are mosques to be seen on every hand, in the district of 'Abbasiyah in the north-east sector of the city you see instead churches; and a large modern cathedral is foremost among them. 'Abbasiyah is the home of most of Cairo's half million or so Coptic Christians, who consider themselves the true descendants of the pharaonic Egyptians. The Coptic language, still used in parts of their church liturgy, is a dialect of ancient Egyptian.

The relation between Muslims and Copts during the centuries of their co-existence in Cairo has been complex. The Copts (the name is derived from the Greek "Aegyptos", meaning Egyptian) were the original occupants of Egypt, conquered by the invading Arab armies in 641. Under the Byzantine Empire the Copts had suffered persecution for their unorthodox beliefs. They therefore looked upon the invading Arabs as liberators, a fact that greatly contributed to the Arab success.

The Christians—and Jews—were generally well treated by the Muslims, unlike the pagans, who were presented with a stark choice between

In the glow of a lamp bearing Coptic crosses, a splendidly robed priest declaims from a pulpit in the ancient Mu'allaqah Church, founded in the south of Cairo during the 4th Century. Egypt's four million or so Copts—the largest religious minority in the city's population—claim to be among the world's earliest Christian communities; they were converted in the 1st Century A.D.

conversion or the sword. As "Peoples of the Book"—that is, those whose scriptures agreed substantially with Muhammad's revelations—they were considered to be entitled to the protection of their Muslim rulers. Under the first Arab conquerors their only major disability was the obligation to pay a substantial poll-tax, from which Muslims were exempt. This liability was enough to ensure many conversions to Islam; the Coptic community that survived was composed of stubborn adherents to the old faith.

In early times the Copts were often employed as administrators by the nomadic Arabs, who had little experience in governing a settled, permanent community. Today, Copts are found in all walks of life, from the poor garbage collectors who live in outlying shanty towns to wealthy doctors and lawyers. Over the centuries, the moral and social life of Copts and Muslims has come to be similar, especially among the poor; but the Copts remain a distinct community, reckoning their religious holidays by the solar calendar, not the Muslim lunar system, and living for the most part in their own quarters of the city.

Apart from 'Abbasiyah, the most Coptic region of Cairo is the area of Misr al-Qadimah—the site of the original city that pre-dated the Muslim invasion. There the remains of the ancient Roman fort called Babylon still contain some of the oldest churches in the world, dating from the 4th and 5th Centuries. The most famous of these is the Mu'allaqah Church—the "Hanging" Church, so-called because it was built above the lofty gatehouse of the fort. Even today, when the ground has risen about 20 feet above the level of Roman times, one reaches the church by climbing a tall flight of steps. The interior has a close and intimate feeling, in spite of modern restorations. The classical columns of the nave arcades were decorated with ghostly figures of saints, of which a few traces remain.

In this Coptic church, no less than in the mosques of Islam, I was acutely aware of the centuries of past belief that lie behind the practices of today. I myself have always been tempted by the theory that faint remnants of pharaonic practices are discernible in some of today's observances. The picnics at the family tombs and the distribution of food to the poor, for example, are in all likelihood versions of the pharaonic practice of burying food and other necessities with the dead, for life in the afterworld. By the same token, the recitation of the *muqri'* could seem to resemble the formulae by which the priests of Memphis, Heliopolis and Thebes ensured the survival of the souls of the dead.

I found such relics of the ancient past strangely impressive, but hardly surprising. I doubt if there is another country on earth that has absorbed so many different traditions and blended them so successfully into a unique, coherent whole. In Egypt, both Christianity and Islam are heirs to one of the oldest civilizations created by man. Whether they are aware of it or not, this heritage survives in the religious life of Cairo's present-day citizens, just as surely and indestructibly as in the Pyramids.

Waiting for a bus, a small group of Cairenes of different generations exemplify the city's wide range of sartorial styles, from the most rustic to those that would pa⋅

The Rural Influence

remarked in any Western city. The man in the foreground makes a typical compromise, wearing his Western-style overcoat on top of his white cotton galabiyah.

Like other Third World capitals, Cairo harbours a society in transition: traditional and modern, urban and rural, Eastern and Western values interact in complex patterns that show themselves in fascinating variations of dress and behaviour. But even while many Cairenes respond to the allure of Western lifestyles and citified sophistication, the huge influx of peasants from the surrounding country constantly renews the influence of rural conservatism. Many an office worker who wears Western shirt and trousers to work will don the *galabiyah*—Egypt's age-old, nightgown-like costume—at home in the evening; while a woman who dresses in subdued black, with head and arms covered as Muslim custom requires, may nonetheless reveal by subtle differences—wrists uncovered, perhaps, or neck exposed —that she is a seasoned city-dweller and not a shy new arrival.

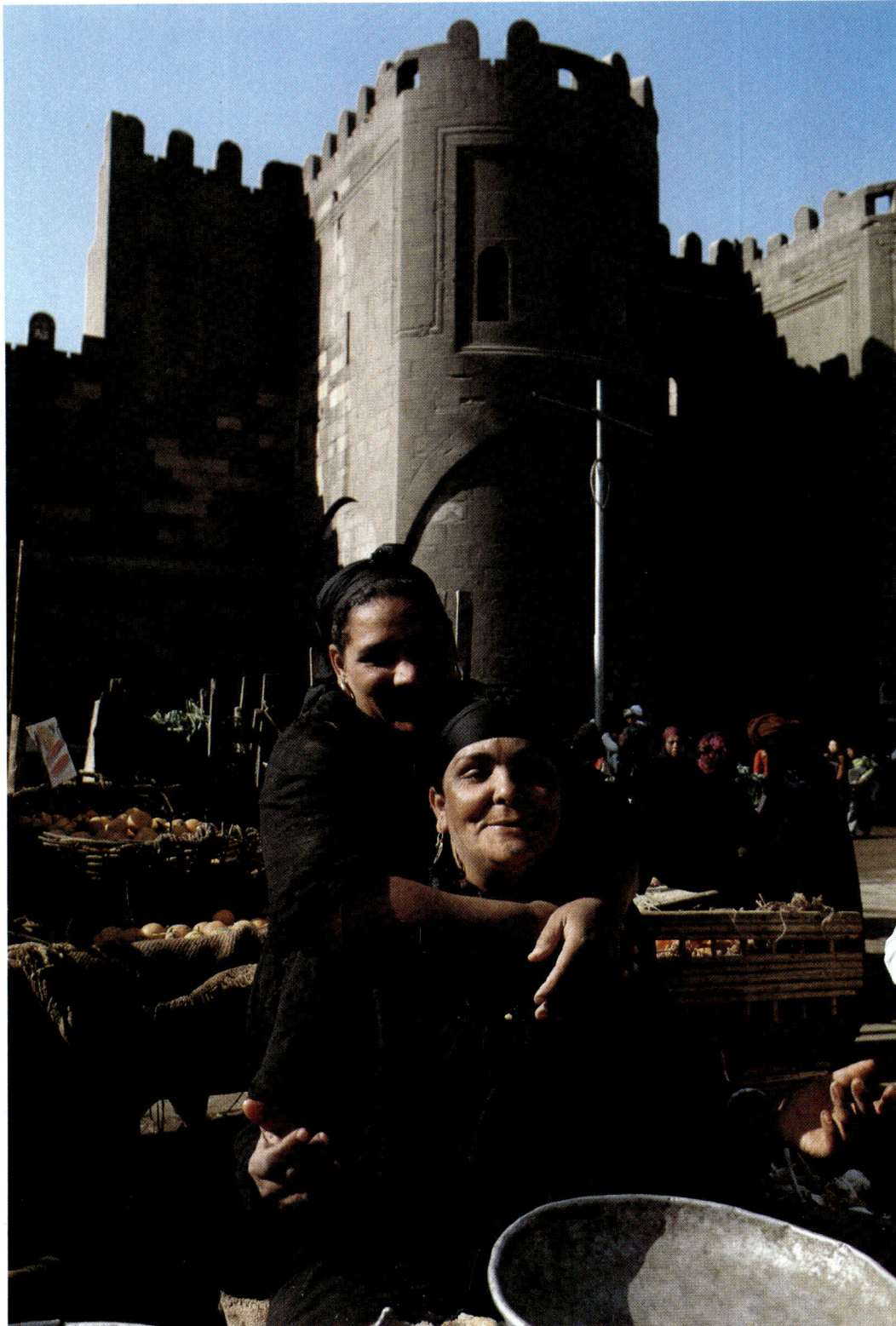

Two stall-holders near the city's medieval walls demonstrate the confidence typical of seasoned market folk.

Exhibiting the grace of a past epoch, an aged woman in a head-dress covered with a delicate gauze scarf passes the time waiting for a friend in southern Cairo.

Obviously at home in the city streets, a young match-seller radiates charm and style-consciousness.

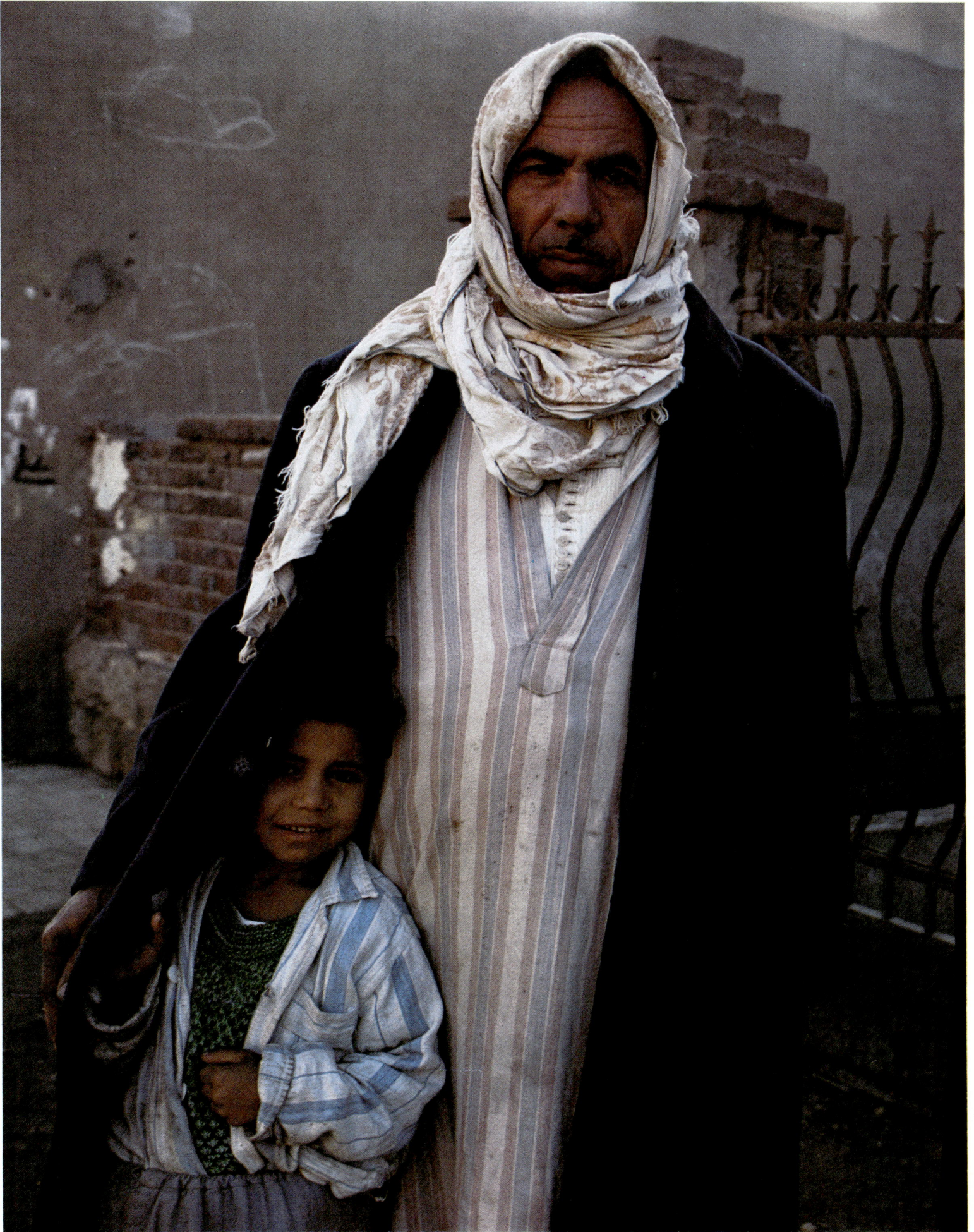

On the outskirts of Cairo near Gizah, a shy little boy from the countryside seeks warming parental protection as he peeps out from his father's overcoat.

Transacting business in Cairo's camel market, merchants from Upper Egypt are distinguished by the enveloping costume—and fierce mien—of desert-dwellers.

4

Under Europe's Sway

On January 26, 1952—a day that has passed into history as "Black Saturday"—the people of Cairo took to the streets. Organized by militant nationalists, citizens rampaged through the European quarters of the capital, burning and looting foreign-owned property. This outburst of xenophobia—a curtain-raiser to the full-blooded Revolution of July 1952 —was a reaction against 150 years of European exploitation of Egypt, and led to the destruction of some 400 buildings: hotels, offices, shops and restaurants. The most notable casualty was the world-famous Shepheard's Hotel, a century-old symbol of foreign domination.

Today, on the Corniche overlooking the Nile, you can find a modern luxury block called Shepheard's Hotel; but apart from its name, this hotel has nothing in common with its predecessor—a palatial, Italian-style building, with a palm-fringed terrace, that formerly stood on the western side of beautiful Azbakiyah Gardens. The old Shepheard's was the most fashionable hotel in the Middle East; a Cairo landmark almost as renowned as the Sphinx itself; and a home-from-home for thousands of Allied officers who were billeted there during the two world wars.

On "Black Saturday", barman Joe Scialon served drinks free of charge in the Long Bar. The management wanted to divert any guests who might be alarmed by the sounds of demonstrators chanting anti-British slogans outside; they had known demonstrations before that were soon brought under control, and it was never the way at Shepheard's to allow a crisis to disturb the well-ordered routine. But shortly after lunch, Molotov cocktails were hurled into the lobby. Rioters invaded the grill-room and demolished the grand piano. The hotel quickly became a raging inferno. By late evening, when Egyptian troops belatedly intervened to restore order, Cairo's favourite haven for foreigners had been reduced to a smouldering shell, with the loss of two lives.

Shepheard's Hotel was a more appropriate target for Cairo's rioting nationalists than perhaps they realized. It stood on a site that had been occupied some 150 years before by a brand-new palace built for Muhammad Bay al-Alfi, one of Egypt's Mamluk rulers. There, in 1798, Western imperialism made its first appearance in Egypt with the arrival of Napoleon Bonaparte, who commandeered the newly built palace for his official headquarters. For the next century and a half, Europeans were to constitute an increasingly intrusive alien presence in Cairo.

Napoleon's visit was brief—less than 14 months—but it had a lasting effect on relations between Egypt and Europe. The 29-year-old General,

In a contemporary French engraver's idealized representation, Napoleon Bonaparte receives a delegation of religious leaders presenting him with the keys of Cairo. Victory came after Napoleon's rout of the Mamluks at the Battle of the Pyramids in 1798. British and Turkish military pressure forced the French to abandon Egypt after three years, but the short-lived occupation set a pattern for European intrusion that was to be sustained for 150 years.

fresh from his astonishing victories over the Austrian armies, had persuaded the rulers of revolutionary France that the most effective way to strike at their arch-enemy, the British, was to occupy Egypt and thus threaten the route to India. "I was full of dreams," he told a friend later. "I saw myself founding a religion, marching into Asia, riding an elephant, a turban on my head, and in my hand a new Koran that I would have composed to suit my needs." This egotistical vision did not, however, long survive Napoleon's face-to-face contact with the reality of the Middle East.

Egypt in the 18th Century was a somnolent backwater, still nominally a province of the Ottoman Turks who had conquered the country in 1517. However, so negligent was the rule of the pashas (in effect, viceroys) sent from Istanbul, the Ottoman capital, that the Mamluks—still numerous in the army, civil service and provincial administrations—remained the real power in the land. They had continued their age-old private feuds and, amid the chaos, Egypt's economic and cultural life had withered.

Napoleon defeated the Mamluks at the Battle of the Pyramids and, in July 1798, entered Cairo at the head of an army of 38,000. His elaborate expeditionary force included a hundred savants—botanists, astronomers, cartographers, archaeologists and artists—with whose support he intended to develop a new colony of dazzling brilliance for France. Yet, only a few weeks after his arrival, Napoleon's grandiose dreams were shattered when Britain's Admiral Nelson sailed into the Bay of Abu Qir, near Alexandria, and overwhelmed the French fleet, thus marooning the invading army.

Undaunted, Napoleon set about bringing civilization to this backward land. The population of Cairo had sunk to a mere 300,000 and the city now, as one of the French officers wrote, presented a depressing spectacle of "narrow, unpaved and dirty streets, dark houses that are falling to pieces, public buildings that look like dungeons, shops that look like stables, an atmosphere full of dust and rubbish".

Napoleon began his crash programme of reforms by introducing municipal government to Cairo in the form of the so-called "Divan"—a council comprising sheikhs, lawyers and Islamic theologians. Then, more ambitiously, he organized the "General Divan": an assembly of representatives from the various Egyptian provinces. Outside the capital, canals were cleared, windmills erected, and flood-control works undertaken on the Nile. New hospitals and libraries were begun in Cairo, its streets were cleared of rotting garbage, and the corruption and brutality of public life markedly reduced. Yet, remarkably little of permanent value was achieved, simply because the Egyptians stubbornly resisted these brusque, alien reforms. The ruling rich resented French attempts to break up, literally overnight, their traditional system of feudal land tenure; they resented laws that denied them their age-old freedom to throw rubbish into the streets, or to ensure the success of their transactions with government officials by the offering of gifts (which the French insisted on condemning

Fashionable tourists wintering in Cairo in 1907
take their ease on the terrace of Shepheard's
Hotel, the favourite rendezvous of the wealthy
Americans and Europeans who visited Egypt
in ever-increasing numbers from the mid-19th
Century onwards. Founded by an Englishman in
the 1840s and later rebuilt, the hotel became
the symbol of foreign privilege in Cairo, and was
burnt down by Egyptian nationalists in 1952.

as "bribes"); and, not least, they despised the way French women went
unveiled in public and generally asserted themselves in a way at odds with
the customs of Muslim society.

In August 1799, a discouraged Bonaparte returned to France in a
frigate that had survived Nelson's attack. Trapped in Cairo, his army was
harassed from within by a popular uprising and later surrounded by Turks
and Mamluks massed in readiness to attack. In March 1801, the additional
threat of a newly arrived British military force compelled the French to
surrender the beleaguered city; they were given 50 days to quit the
country. The British restored the Turks and their Mamluk officials to power;
and some months later, satisfied that the route to India was now safe,
they departed from Egypt. But they were eventually to return.

Bonaparte's expedition had been a military disaster, yet it gave Europeans
a new awareness of the strategic significance of Egypt, situated as it is at
the hinge of the African and Asian continents. At the same time, it introduced the ideas of the French Enlightenment to a seemingly static Muslim
society. Egypt—and especially its capital—could never be the same again.

One immediate effect of the French expedition was to weaken fatally
the power of the Mamluks. The vacuum this left was quickly filled by a
young Ottoman officer named Muhammad 'Ali, from Macedonia in what
is now Greece. He had come to Egypt in 1801 with an Albanian detachment of the Turkish expeditionary force that had been despatched to expel
the French, and rose to prominence in the period of chaos that followed

the departure of the European forces. The people of Cairo, tired of bloody anarchy, united behind their religious leaders to choose Muhammad 'Ali —a foreigner himself, but all-importantly a Muslim—as their governor. In 1805, the Ottoman Sultan reluctantly confirmed him as Pasha of Egypt, thereby establishing a dynasty that lasted 147 years; it did not come to an end until 1952, when Muhammad 'Ali's portly great-great-grandson, Faruq, the ninth ruler of the line, was turned off the throne.

Any challenge that the surviving Mamluks might have presented to the new Pasha was removed at one fell swoop on March 1, 1811, when Muhammad 'Ali invited nearly 500 of their leaders to a grand reception in Cairo's Citadel. He received them most graciously, allaying any suspicions they may have had. As they left, mounted in all their finery, to ride down the passage between the Citadel's inner and outer gates, Muhammad 'Ali's Albanians, who had been posted on the walls above, opened fire, and then descended to finish off their victims with scimitars. The carnage was horrible. According to an account by an Englishman, James Webster, who visited Cairo when the events were still fresh in people's memories: "The Citadel itself looked like a hideous slaughterhouse, newly deluged with the blood of victims, and overstrown [*sic*] with a multitude of reeking carcasses. Dead steeds lay confusedly along the streets with their golden caparisons soiled in the filthy compound of dirt and gore; their knights, some with limbs hacked off, others without their heads, still clenching their scimitars with the last despairing, yet desperate grasp of death, were flung near their war-horses, prostrate in a black puddle of their own life-blood."

Throughout the country, Mamluk houses were ransacked and their occupants, totalling about 5,000, were killed. A few Mamluks escaped to the Sudan, and a handful survived in Egypt; but finally, after almost 600 years, their power was broken, never to be re-established.

Muhammad 'Ali was now master in his own house and set out to create a powerful Egypt that would be independent of Istanbul. Although himself illiterate, the Pasha greatly admired European civilization as epitomized at that time by France. French influence and expertise were soon making themselves felt all over Egypt. To help train his new army, largely composed of conscripted and undisciplined fellahin, he employed many of the brilliant French officers left unemployed by the collapse of the Napoleonic Empire. With French help, European-style schools and factories were built; although primitive, they were the first of their kind in Egypt. French engineers were invited to Egypt to build a network of canals and irrigation dams; and hundreds of young Egyptians were sent to Paris to study industry, engineering, medicine and agriculture. Much of Egypt was transformed into a vast government-owned farm, and a million new acres were eventually brought under the plough.

Most importantly of all, in 1822 Muhammad 'Ali was persuaded by a French agricultural expert, M. Jumel, to plant cotton of the long-staple variety in Egypt. More than any other single event, the introduction of cotton-growing enabled the Pasha to realize his dreams of involving his country in the booming economy of Europe. Long-staple cotton is particularly suitable for weaving fine fabrics, and the initial experiments with cultivating it in Egypt proved so successful that the fellahin were compelled to plant the crop all over the Delta. Refusal to do so meant being bastinadoed, or press-ganged into the Pasha's ever-growing army; by the middle of the 19th Century, Egypt's export earnings were dependent largely on the country's quarter of a million acres of cotton fields.

All the Pasha's modernizing reforms had one ultimate purpose: to build Egypt into a strong power. The achievements of his army, which numbered 90,000 men at its peak, were certainly impressive: from 1816 to 1818 it conquered central Arabia; in 1821, the Sudan; from 1831 to 1833, Syria; and by 1839 it was threatening the Ottoman Empire itself. Alarmed at this upset in the international balance of power, the major European nations launched a diplomatic offensive to stem Egyptian expansion. The Treaty of London, concluded in 1841 by Great Britain, Austria, Russia and Prussia, finally put an end to Muhammad 'Ali's imperial ambitions by forcing him to hand back Syria to the Ottoman Sultan, and to reduce his army to 18,000 men.

At home, the Pasha's harsh maintenance of law and order had given Egypt a degree of internal security it had not known for four centuries, enabling Western travellers to visit the country in reasonable comfort and safety. This they did in ever-increasing numbers; for one effect of Napoleon's expedition had been to create a boundless interest in all things Egyptian. Between 1808 and 1825, Napoleon's returned brigade of savants had completed and published their findings in the *Description de l'Egypte*, 24 magnificent folio volumes—10 of text and 14 of illustrations —that described for the first time the spectacular riches of the pharaonic civilization and inspired a new discipline: Egyptology. In the wake of Napoleon's scholars came two other remarkable Frenchmen: Jean François Champollion, who between 1822 and his death in 1832 deciphered the ancient Egyptians' hieroglyphic script and thus unlocked the secrets of pharaonic writings; and Auguste Mariette, who first excavated the Old Kingdom tombs, dating from the 30th Century B.C., at Saqqarah, the great necropolis 20 miles south of Cairo.

There ensued a scramble for antiquities in which serious archaeologists competed with tomb-robbing profiteers. A Swiss, Johann Burckhardt, rediscovered far up the Nile near Aswan the stupendous temple of Abu Simbal, with its 67-foot-high statues of the Pharaoh Ramses II; an Italian, Giovanni Belzoni, formerly a circus strong man, excavated many of the pharaonic sites in Upper Egypt; and an Englishman, Colonel Richard Howard-Vyse, used gunpowder to gain access to the Pyramids and bored holes in the Sphinx to find out if it were hollow. But there were

In 1899, a 22½-foot-high statue of Ferdinand de Lesseps, the far-sighted French diplomat who master-minded the building of the Suez Canal between 1854 and 1869, awaits installation at Port Sa'id, the canal's northern mouth. The bronze colossus, commemorating de Lesseps' achievement in linking the Mediterranean and Red seas, was dynamited by an anti-Western mob in 1956 when President Nasser repossessed the canal from its foreign shareholders.

many others who took unscrupulous advantage of the West's passionate interest in the mysteries of ancient Egypt. Henry Salt, the British Consul in Cairo from 1816 to 1827, made a personal fortune from antiquities shipped to Europe in large quantities. The painted limestone bust of Queen Nefertiti, dating from about 1350 B.C. and found at Tall al-Amarna in Upper Egypt—a work which has long symbolized pharaonic Egypt to millions throughout the world and is now the prize of the Egyptian Museum in West Berlin—is believed to have been slipped out in the imperial German diplomatic bag just before the First World War. The great century of Egyptian discoveries was to reach its climax in 1922 when the British expedition of Lord Carnarvon and Howard Carter found the treasure of Tutankhamun in the Valley of the Kings at Thebes.

In addition to the archaeologists, an ever-increasing proportion of the travellers on their way to India chose to take the overland route through Muhammad 'Ali's Egypt; and when a railway link (the first in either Africa or Asia) was opened from Alexandria to Cairo via Suez in 1852, the stream of visitors became a flood.

Samuel Shepheard's celebrated hotel was their main crossroads. Shepheard had begun his career as a pastry-cook on board a Peninsular & Oriental liner, but he was dumped ashore at Suez in 1842 when he sided with shipmates who mutinied over their primitive conditions. After spending some years as a hotel manager in Cairo, he was in 1849 given permission by 'Abbas (who that year had succeeded his grandfather Muhammad 'Ali as ruler of Egypt) to convert Napoleon's one-time headquarters—the old palace of Muhammad Bay al-Alfi in the district of Azbakiyah—into a hotel. In the 1890s the original building, described by an American diplomat as "a grim old barrack", was demolished and replaced by a new hotel in a florid Italianate style that boasted a magnificent "Moorish hall" adorned with striped horseshoe arches, honey-coloured alabaster tables and fine red Persian carpets, and a ballroom in the Louis XV manner, lit by an enormous crystal chandelier.

During the closing decades of the 19th Century the rich, famous and influential of Europe and America—whether on vacation or in transit to the Far East—flocked to Shepheard's; indeed, the management was frequently obliged to turn would-be guests away. A typical day at the hotel began with a vast breakfast, served by *safragis* (waiters) in crimson and gold embroidered jackets and white pantaloons. Guests could then hire a guide and a donkey from among the vast crowd of hopefuls that milled about outside Shepheard's, and set off for a mounted tour of the Cairo bazaars or the Pyramids. Early evening brought a dinner that could last several hours, accompanied by the finest French wines. Later, the Louis XV ballroom was often the scene of a glittering fancy-dress ball, offering the curious spectacle of European celebrities dressed as Cairo water-sellers or Japanese samurai. In the famous Long Bar, young British

Some of Cook's staff in 1869 gather outside their Cairo office, then located at Shepheard's Hotel.

Cook's Tourism

Commercial tourism in Egypt dates from 1869, when an Englishman, Thomas Cook, organized a tour of the Holy Land that took in a visit to Cairo and the newly built Suez Canal. By the turn of the century, Cook's Tours—headed by the founder's son, John Mason Cook—employed a huge force of guides, interpreters and porters for excursions to the Pyramids or up the Nile. The company's success was based, above all, on the use of specially equipped luxury steamers on the Nile; the floating grand hotels provided their guests with palatial comforts and transported them up-river to within a short donkey ride of many of the spectacular temples and tombs of ancient Egypt.

The "Egypt", one of Cook's fleet of stately river steamers, could carry 430 passengers on a day excursion, or 80 people for the three-week trip 600 miles up the Nile to see the pharaonic temples at Aswan. Accommodation included a spacious lounge (inset) that opened on to the broad promenade deck.

army officers drank and joked, while outside on the terrace other guests sipped their coffee, discussed the latest high-society scandal and watched the moon cast a silver light on the palm trees of Azbakiyah Gardens.

Great events often have trivial causes—and especially so in Egypt, where life-and-death decisions have so often hung on the whim of a powerful pharaoh, pasha or president. The story of the Suez Canal is a case in point. Its construction was made possible by the personal friendship of two men: Ferdinand de Lesseps, the French Consul in Cairo from 1833 to 1837, and Sa'id, younger son of Muhammad 'Ali, who became Pasha of Egypt in 1854. In his youth, Sa'id was, like other princes of his line, inclined to corpulence, a fact which disgusted his father, the old Albanian warrior. The boy was put under a Spartan regime: vigorous exercise and a diet of greens and lentils. He was also forbidden to make any outside visits, except to pay calls on the favoured French Consul; and it was de Lesseps who slaked the pangs of royal hunger by treating the Prince to liberal portions of spaghetti and macaroni.

The Consul's hospitality was amply rewarded when Sa'id unexpectedly came to the viceregal throne following the assassination in July 1854 of his nephew, 'Abbas. De Lesseps, who had been away from Egypt for 17 years, promptly hastened to Cairo. Within five months he had obtained the first concession for the Suez Canal, a visionary but risky enterprise that for a century tied Egypt closely to Europe.

It was to take another 15 years of diplomatic, financial and legal wrangling before the canal was finally completed, in 1869. In the meantime, Sa'id died at the age of 47 and was succeeded by his nephew Isma'il. A well-travelled, European-educated man of immense personal charm, Isma'il was remarkable for his courage and far-sightedness. In 1863, when he came to power, it certainly seemed that Egypt had a bright future. In the United States of America—previously the world's major supplier of long-staple cotton—the Civil War was grinding into its third year without a hint of conclusion, causing the value of Egyptian cotton exports to soar by millions of dollars; the fellahin ate meat and took second wives.

In the spring of 1867 Isma'il was invited by Napoleon III to the *Exposition Universelle* in Paris, an event which was in effect the symbolic unveiling of the renovated city created by the French Emperor's great protégé, Baron Haussmann. Isma'il had known Paris in his youth, when he studied at the Military Academy of St. Cyr; but no memory of that city of narrow, winding streets had prepared him for the new "Haussmannized" Paris, with its broad boulevards, impressive municipal utilities and beautiful parks and public gardens. If medieval Paris could be thus transformed, he decided, then so too could Cairo.

By dint of raising loans from the great banking houses of Europe—and wringing yet more taxes out of the luckless Egyptian fellahin—Isma'il

launched a massive development scheme aimed at creating a "Paris on the Nile" in time for the celebrations that would mark the opening of the Suez Canal. A new façade of attractive, European-style villas was constructed on reclaimed land on the east bank of the Nile, screening off the shabbiness of medieval Cairo further east. Wide boulevards with sidewalks were laid out, and adjacent land was given free to princes and wealthy merchants who agreed to build luxurious villas with gardens. Barrilet-Deschamps, the French landscape designer who had assisted Haussmann, was brought over to redesign the gardens in the older European quarter of Azbakiyah. A great Opera House, of Lebanese wood and stucco, was built nearby. The result was the creation of two distinct cities side by side: an Egyptian Cairo to the east, a European Cairo to the west.

On Gezirah, a German firm constructed splendid new accommodation for the distinguished foreign guests who would attend the opening of the canal—in effect, a palace for visitors; the rest of the island—hitherto mainly reserved for hunting and agriculture—was laid out with formal gardens. Most importantly for the future of tourism, a great raised highway was constructed from Gizah to the Pyramids, a route previously impassable to wheeled traffic in summer because of the flooding of the Nile.

In November 1869, immediately before the opening of the Suez Canal, Isma'il's newly designed capital witnessed one of the most spectacular celebrations of the 19th Century. The star of the occasion was the Empress Eugénie of France, a distant kinswoman of de Lesseps, who arrived at the head of a glittering train of European royalty that included the Emperor Franz Josef of Austria and the Prince and Princess of Wales. The Empress' suite in the new Gezirah palace was fitted out to resemble her private apartments in the Tuileries. At the Pyramids, which were illuminated after dark by magnesium flares, a wooden chalet was constructed to accommodate her overnight. In Cairo itself, there were innumerable banquets and receptions; and a gala performance of Verdi's *Rigoletto* inaugurated the new Opera House. The opera was the only attraction that did not exactly accord with Isma'il's grandiose plans; the performance should have been the world premiere of *Aïda*, a pharaonic tale especially commissioned for the occasion, but Verdi had not been given sufficient time to complete it.

The visit of the portly but still handsome Empress Eugénie was a landmark in Isma'il's reign because it seemed to mark his acceptance into the ranks of European royalty. It was talked of long after both she and Isma'il had left the international stage. The widow of a former Egyptian Ambassador to Czechoslovakia in the 1930s once told me how her grandmother, a lady-in-waiting in Isma'il's harem, had been present when the Empress came to pay her respects. There was a problem of protocol since it was felt to be unfitting for the Muslim ladies to curtsey to the Empress, thus implying obedience to a Christian sovereign. At the same time, everyone wished to show her the respect due to Cairo's most distinguished visitor.

Australian troops, on leave in Cairo during the First World War, crowd the trams returning them to their base near the Gizah Pyramids. Free spending by Allied soldiers brought a measure of prosperity to the capital during the war, but the rowdy behaviour of many of the troops—stationed in Egypt to protect it from the Turks, allies of Germany—angered and alienated Egyptian public opinion.

My friend's grandmother suggested a compromise, by which the Egyptian ladies kissed the Empress' hand, but without curtseying.

With a capital half transformed into a Western metropolis and a country with all the surface aspects of an industrialized 19th-Century state—roads, railways, factories, telegraph services—Isma'il felt able to make (in French) his most quoted remark: "My country is no longer in Africa; we are now part of Europe."

The Westernized districts of Cairo could with reason be described as part of Europe. They had an enormous population of Europeans: as many as 80,000 had arrived in Egypt in 1865 alone, some to visit, but many to settle and open businesses. Owing to the discoveries of archaeologists and the exotic accounts of travel writers, the city now had a booming tourist trade as well as its usual flow of travellers in transit. One observer after another attempted to do justice to the Pyramids. One of the most renowned was Mark Twain, who visited Cairo in 1867 on an excursion with more than 60 other Americans. His account, published in his popular book, *Innocents Abroad*, made his name famous in Cairo; well into the 20th Century, travellers to the Pyramids found they were being offered rides on donkeys called "Marka Twain".

Egyptian tourism was greatly boosted by an Englishman who epitomized the twin Victorian qualities of high-minded idealism and commercial opportunism. He was Thomas J. Cook, a temperance campaigner and railway-tour operator who may justly be called the Father of the Package Tour. Cook, who was born in 1808, began his career by organizing railway excursions for teetotallers in the English Midlands. His business soon expanded to include tours to France, Switzerland and Italy. In 1868 he made his first visit to Cairo and, on his return to England, immediately began organizing a tour to Egypt and the Holy Land for a contingent of just 32 ladies and gentlemen. It was the beginning of commercial tourism in the Middle East. By the end of the century Cook's company had virtually monopolized Egypt's burgeoning tourist industry.

A writer in the English *Blackwood's Magazine* observed at the time that Thomas Cook and Son, and not the Khedive (the title by which the Pasha of Egypt was known from 1867 onwards), was the real governor of Egypt. He went on to say: "Cook's representative is the first person you meet in Egypt, and you go on meeting him. He sees you in, he sees you through, he sees you out. You see the back of a native turban, long blue gown, red girdle, bare brown legs. 'How truly oriental,' you say. Then he turns round, and you see 'Cook's Porter' emblazoned across his breast. 'You travel Cook, sir,' he grins; 'all right.' And it is all right."

The secret of Cook's success was that he created a micro-environment where the tourist, isolated from abrasive contacts with a strange people in a strange land, could feel thoroughly at home. The specially built steamers that made the 1,200-mile round trip up the Nile from Cairo to the First Cataract and back had all the comforts of an Edwardian club. There were bridge parties and tea-parties, a comfortable little reading room, and a promenade deck furnished with easy chairs and tables, and fitted with a windscreen. Newspapers and mail arrived from England each day. The touring itself was a leisurely affair—nothing more strenuous than the occasional excursion ashore, including a donkey ride.

Few of the *kukiyat*, as Cook's Nile steamers were known to Egyptians, survive. However, I was once lucky enough to be invited on board one of them which now serves as a private houseboat, permanently moored alongside Gezirah. Although it was high summer, the promenade was pleasantly cool, fanned as it was by the breezes of the Nile. Those Victorians, I thought as I sank into an easy chair and sipped a glass of wine, understood the sensual delights of Egypt much better than the modern hotel developers who blot out the sounds of the river with piped music and ruin the gentle touch of the night with air-conditioning.

By 1869 Isma'il was world-famous but already deeply in debt. In the collapse of the cotton boom that followed the end of the American Civil War, he was forced by his creditors to accept British and French financial control; and in 1879 he was deposed.

Resentful of foreign intervention, liberal politicians and Egyptian-born officers had by 1881 allied themselves in a nationalist movement with the

Late in 1942, a group of British servicewomen take time off from their military duties to have their photograph taken on the forepaw of the Sphinx, the great pharaonic figure that guards the ceremonial approach to one of the Pyramids at Gizah. Although Cairo did not suffer serious bombing during the Second World War, the Sphinx was protected against any casual air-raid damage by the erection of a brick wall at its front and a sandbag cushion beneath its chin.

On leave in Cairo during the Second World War, a British serviceman enjoys a shoe-shine. Adopted as the British headquarters in the Middle East, the city offered Allied troops a welcome respite from the desert war; since, in spite of the British presence, Egypt was officially a neutral country, many luxury items rationed or unobtainable in war-torn Europe remained freely available there.

rallying cry "Egypt for the Egyptians"; for it a spokesman was found in the shambling but dignified figure of Colonel Ahmad 'Arabi, a man of peasant origins. 'Arabi eloquently expressed the growing national consciousness of his people and, as Minister for War, wielded effective control over Egypt for more than a year. But he was a mediocre leader; in 1882, fearful that nationalists would repudiate Isma'il's debts and seize the Suez Canal, Britain landed an expeditionary force that easily defeated 'Arabi's hastily recruited army at Tall al-Kabir, 50 miles north-east of Cairo.

The British occupation that followed was supposed to be temporary, to protect European financial interests and guard the route to India until the restoration of law and order. In fact, it lasted for more than 70 years, in an unwritten system that came to be known as the "Veiled Protectorate".

For almost a quarter of a century, from 1883 to 1907, the key post of British Agent or Consul-General was held by one remarkable man, Sir Evelyn Baring, later Lord Cromer. A member of a famous banking family, he was the archetypal imperial administrator; over-confident to the point of arrogance (earning him the nickname "over-Baring"), opinionated to the point of bigotry, but nevertheless a highly efficient administrator who sought to improve the lot of the poor and the oppressed. Cromer was a firm believer in Britain's "civilizing mission", as a bearer of Christian civilization, to rule over "subject races". He believed in spending money only for a solid material return and therefore abolished the free schooling instituted by Muhammad 'Ali and Isma'il. Young Egyptians who secured a university education (usually in France) were free to speak or write their opinions, but were denied political power. Cromer considered them irritating but harmless and termed them contemptuously "Gallicized" Egyptians.

In financial terms, Cromer's rule was an outstanding success. Egypt's enormous debts were paid off and the whip was no longer used to collect taxes from the fellahin. The building of a giant dam at Aswan and the restoration of the old French-built irrigation system by British engineers brought great benefits for agriculture. But Egypt's growing prosperity served not only to widen the gap between rich and poor, but also to place the country more firmly in foreign hands. By 1914, more than 90 per cent of the capital of Egyptian joint-stock companies was foreign-owned. Banking and commerce were almost entirely in the hands of the "Levantines": Greeks, Italians, Syrians and Armenians.

The British Army was stationed in the Qasr al-Nil barracks, close to the present-day site of the Hilton Hotel. But the barracks, a stark, forbidding building, was treated as nothing more than a dormitory, especially by the officers. The British officers' spiritual home—deliberately isolated from workaday Cairo—was across the river, in the spacious parkland of the Gezirah Sporting Club. There, they amused themselves with tennis, croquet, polo, golf and horse-racing, and sipped their drinks at sundown under the flaming jacarandas. They rarely ventured away from the island, except perhaps to go duck-shooting in the teeming marshes of Fayyum and Lake Maryut, near Alexandria.

This was the Cairo that my grandfather found when he arrived in 1897. He had been infected by dreams of Empire and longed to become a regular army officer. But, unlike most of his schoolmates, he was too poor to do so. In those days the fashionable regiments of the British Army expected their officers to keep up appearances by, for example, acquiring a good horse and spending freely in the officers' mess. Army pay was quite inadequate to cover these expenses, since it was assumed that any self-respecting officer would have a private income. By dint of perseverance, however, my grandfather managed to get a commission in the local militia, a group of part-time soldiers who received military training on perhaps one day a month. He skipped most of his training and, without waiting for permission, sailed for Egypt, where he got himself attached to the anti-slavery detachment of the Egyptian Camel Corps—an unpromising position for an ambitious man, for the chances of action were pretty remote.

But in 1898 he was sent to join General Kitchener, Sirdar (Commander-in-Chief) of the Anglo-Egyptian army that was confronting the forces of the rebellious Sudanese, who 13 years earlier had killed General Gordon at Khartoum. Shortly after Kitchener's victory at Omdurman, the Camel Corps commanded by my grandfather was ordered to join a motley force of Egyptian and Arab troops, who had neither machine guns nor artillery, in an attack on the town of Geddaref. It was a foolhardy venture, but they managed to pull it off. At a crucial point in the battle, my grandfather helped to save the day with a camel charge and rescued a wounded Egyptian officer, keeping the enemy at bay with his pistol.

When he returned to Cairo after the campaign, he found three missives waiting for him. One was a letter from the War Office in London, announcing his dismissal from the militia for being absent without leave. The second was a telegram from his mother, telling him that he had been awarded the Victoria Cross, on Lord Kitchener's recommendation, for his part in the Battle of Geddaref. The third was another letter from the War Office, offering him the thing he most longed for—a commission in a regular army regiment. His elation over this last news was soon crushed for, after a month's hectic participation in the racing and polo at Cairo, he returned to London, where the commission was withdrawn on medical grounds. Although he was an imposing man, well over six feet tall, my grandfather was not surprisingly somewhat emaciated after his Sudanese experiences; but the army doctors decided that his height was too great for his weight. It took the personal intervention of Queen Victoria to overcome that particular piece of military red tape.

The British imperial system was riddled with snobbery. Even permanent British residents of Cairo rarely mixed socially with native Egyptians or the

Carrying banners attacking the oppressive nature of British colonial rule, Egyptian citizens parade through Cairo's streets in one of the many huge nationalist demonstrations staged between 1946 and 1952. Egyptian hostility to Britain—exacerbated by the British refusal to withdraw their garrison in the Suez Canal Zone —culminated in the Revolution of 1952.

wealthier Levantines; moreover, contemporary accounts give the distinct impression that many of the civilian English administrators would scarcely consort with one another.

This was the heyday of those strange hybrids, "Smith Bey" and "Jones Pasha"—mustachioed English gentlemen who, along with their Armenian, Jewish, Coptic and Muslim colleagues in the administration, wore the tarboosh, the red fez that throughout the Ottoman Empire denoted an *effendi*, or civil servant. Nominally, they were employees of the Sultan, serving in the government ministries, the railways, the irrigation department, the Egyptian army and other sections of the state machine. Actually, of course, they were furthering the interests of Britain and, where there was no obvious conflict, those of the European banks and governments that had acquired shares in the great joint-stock company that now constituted the Egyptian State.

Within the British élite there was a complicated pecking order. Generally, Finance took precedence over the Egyptian army; and these were followed in turn by Interior, Justice, Irrigation and Public Works. Below them came Egyptian Railways and, lastly, Education or P.I. (Public Instruction). Members of this latter organization, being "intellectuals", were barely accorded a livelihood. Their lowly status was summed up in a contemporary joke about two friends from the same public school and university who ended up, respectively, in Finance and P.I. Having grasped the social situation in all its clarity, Finance failed to contact Education for several months; but one day they accidentally came face to face outside Cairo's exclusive Turf Club and recognition was unavoidable.

"Hello," said Finance heartily. "I'd no idea you were out here. What department are you in?"

"Well," said Education meekly, "as a matter of fact I'm in the P.I., but please don't mention it at home as I've told my people I'm playing the piano in a brothel."

In 1914, with the outbreak of the First World War, the veil was at last removed from the British presence; Egypt was formally declared a British Protectorate. Her foremost role was to serve as a vast Allied military base and hospital. As the "R and R" centre for the troops, Cairo prospered greatly. Officers forced up the prices of antiques—real or faked—and handicrafts in the bazaar area. Soldiers lavished their money, and affections, on the painted ladies, costing a shilling a time, who frequented the Azbakiyah fishmarkets (known as the Wasa', meaning "open land") across the way from Shepheard's Hotel, or who displayed their charms under the Paris-style colonnades of the nearby thoroughfares of Clot Bay and Shari' Muhammad 'Ali.

In Cairo, the best-paying customers of prostitutes were the Australian and New Zealand troops stationed at Mena House Hotel near the

On July 28, 1952, Egyptian revolutionary troops seal off King Faruq's 'Abdin Palace following the bloodless coup d'état carried out in Cairo by Gamal Abdel Nasser and his clandestine nationalist group, the Free Officers. The King, residing in Alexandria at the time, was forced to abdicate and immediately went into exile in Italy.

Pyramids. It has been estimated that they contributed between £3,000 and £4,000 per day to such insalubrious establishments as the "Melbourne Buffet" and "Sydney Saloon", lured there by such enticing signs as "Squar Dunkum Feed" or the unintentionally candid "Australians Done Here". Many complained of being cheated, robbed, or of having their drinks spiked with drugs; and a few days before the departure of the Australian and New Zealand troops for Gallipoli in 1915 there was a grand settling of scores in the Wasa'. Painted ladies, pianos and furniture rained down on the streets as the men tore through the brothels. The majority of the quarter was burnt to the ground, much to the approval of the respectable guests at Shepheard's, for whom the outrageous goings-on at the fish-market had been a constant affront.

Egyptian nationalists had been obliged to maintain a low profile during the years of the First World War; but all the while they planned resistance to the British and, when the war ended, a tall, eloquent lawyer named Sa'ad Zaghlul emerged as their leader. In 1918 his request for a *wafd* (delegation) to present Egypt's case for independence in London and at the Paris Peace Conference was refused by the British government, which brusquely exiled Zaghlul to Malta. It was the signal for the 1919 uprising: massive strikes and demonstrations, and pitched battles between British troops and the people of Cairo, succeeded in paralyzing the country for a time. To restore order, the British sent out Lord Allenby, victor over the Turks during the war, followed by a mission—boycotted by all the Egyptian

politicians—to work out a new constitution. Finally, in 1922, after two more years of civil disorder, Britain unilaterally declared the end of the Protectorate and recognized Egypt as an independent constitutional monarchy.

Yet, it was independence in little more than name. Conflict simmered continuously between the King, the Wafd (the nationalist party that had won the Egyptian elections in 1924) and the British. In 1924, Sir Lee Stack, the British Commander-in-Chief of the Egyptian army and Governor-General of the Sudan, was assassinated in broad daylight by terrorists as he drove through Cairo. By the 1930s, students demonstrating against the British had become a familiar sight in the city streets. One of their leaders was a tall, dark youth named Gamal Abdel Nasser.

In 1936, however, Mussolini's aggressive expansion in Africa brought the British and the Wafdists temporarily closer, and the outlook seemed more promising. In April of that year, King Fu'ad died and was succeeded by his handsome, smiling, 18-year-old son Faruq, who was given a wildly enthusiastic welcome when he returned from school in England. At last it seemed that Egypt had emerged from its semi-colonial status. But when the Second World War broke out, Britain invoked the terms of the 1936 treaty and reoccupied the country.

Egypt was technically neutral during the war; many luxuries unobtainable in Europe—such as steaks, French wine, cigarettes and belly-dancers—were in plentiful supply. Yet, Cairo was really a wartime capital, the centre of Britain's G.H.Q. for the Middle East, commanding the armies of

North Africa, the eastern Mediterranean and western Asia. At one point in early 1942, Axis Forces under General Rommel—a hero to many Egyptians—were within a hundred miles of the city.

For the British in Cairo, it was an aristocratic, high-spirited war in which individualism and bureaucracy were mingled in a way that would have been impossible back in Britain. Adventurous society girls stole out from London on forged papers to join, or seek news of, lovers or husbands, or perhaps to make a catch. For unattached women there was a wealth of possible choices: the blue bloods whose connections got them staff jobs away from the front, or the "nobs" of Corps Headquarters and the Long Range Desert Group, who carefully distinguished themselves from mere regimental soldiers by affecting the non-military garb of corduroy trousers and sheepskin jackets.

The Long Range Desert Group was a commando outfit led by the legendary Sterling brothers, Bill and David, two young English officers whose daring exploits behind the enemy lines—where they blew up trucks and petrol dumps, and laid mines along the desert roads—made them the talk of Cairo. Feeling that if one had to fight a war then it should be as dangerous as possible, my father left his regiment, the Rifle Brigade, and joined the group. Their unofficial headquarters was an apartment in Isma'il's stately Garden City, where jagged holes in the walls and ceilings testified to the Sterling brothers' revolver practice.

The other chosen haunt of the select fraternity was, of course, the Long Bar at Shepheard's, where many an armchair commando sought their company. The latter, known as the Short Range Shepheard's Group, were the subject of a famous lampoon:

> We never went west of Gezirah
> We never went north of the Nile
> We never went past the Pyramids
> Out of sight of the Sphinx's smile.
> We fought the war in Shepheard's
> And the Continental Bar.
> We reserved our punch for the Turf Club lunch
> And they gave us the Africa Star.

The Second World War saw the last, exotic flowering of Egypt's ancient regime—also, to a large extent, that of the Old Europe that, elsewhere, disappeared in 1939. Olivia Manning, a British writer who fled before the Nazis from Rumania—where her husband had been a lecturer—and eventually ended up in Cairo, wrote in her book *The Danger Tree*: "Cairo had become the clearing house of Eastern Europe. Kings and princes, heads of state, their followers and hangers-on, free governments with all their officials, everyone who saw himself committed to the Allied cause, had come to live off the charity of the British government. Hotels, restaurants and cafés were loud with the squabbles, rivalries, scandals, exhibitions of importance and hurt feelings that occupied the refugees while they waited for the war to end and the old order to return."

The war ended, but the old order did not come back.

After the war, Egypt needed wise and firm government more than ever; but it was not forthcoming. King Faruq, who by now had degenerated into an obese, sexually voracious monster, was filled with impotent hatred of the British. British troops were withdrawn from Cairo, but remained in the Canal Zone in great strength; and all attempts to reach a final agreement to end the occupation foundered. In 1948 a badly led and ill-equipped Egyptian army was sent to Palestine to prevent the establishment of the new state of Israel. After its ignominious defeat, the recently formed Free Officers, a clandestine nationalist group within the Egyptian army led by Gamal Abdel Nasser, resolved that the system must be changed.

To restore its by-now faded nationalist credentials, the Wafdist government denounced the Anglo-Egyptian Treaty of 1936 and launched a campaign of sabotage and guerrilla attacks against the British forces in the Canal Zone. It was the British retaliation—in particular, the killing of 70 Egyptian police officers in a battle at Isma'iliyah—that led to "Black Saturday". The Egyptian monarchy was doomed. On the night of July 22, 1952, while Faruq was in his summer palace at Alexandria, the Free Officers seized the capital with little difficulty. One of them, named Anwar Sadat, announced the Revolution over Cairo Radio. Egypt was back in the hands of the Egyptians for the first time in 25 centuries.

Among the effects of Shepheard's Hotel that went up in smoke in the great fire, along with the satin drapes, the precious tapestries on the walls and the great Persian carpet, was the treasured visitors' book. It bore the signatures of Theodore Roosevelt, T. E. Lawrence, General Gordon, Douglas Fairbanks Senior, Mary Pickford, Rudyard Kipling, G. B. Shaw, General de Gaulle, Noel Coward and Winston Churchill, not to mention numerous kings and queens and assorted multi-millionaires. With it perished the whole era that it recorded.

The Great Pyramids

Almost obscuring the Great Pyramid behind it, Khafre's smaller tomb looms above that of Menkaure. The lesser tombs (foreground) were for royal relatives.

Throughout Cairo's thousand-year history, visitors have marvelled at the relics of a culture 30 centuries older than the city itself: the three huge Pyramids at Gizah, nine miles to the south-west. And the fascination that springs from the Pyramids' sheer scale is enhanced by tricks of perspective that impart infinite variety to the majestic group of royal tombs. Of Egypt's 80 or so surviving pyramids, most were built in the third millennium B.C. The Gizah trio includes the largest of all: the Great Pyramid of the Pharaoh Khufu, completed in about 2600 B.C. Originally 481 feet high, but now 30 feet shorter after the loss of its outer facing-stones, the Great Pyramid stands in an accurately aligned row with the slightly smaller monument of Khufu's son, Khafre, and the Pyramid of a later successor, Menkaure, whose tomb is less than half the mass of Khafre's.

Dwarfing settlements that straggle towards their bases, the Pyramids of Khufu, Khafre and Menkaure (right to left) rise in splendid symmetry above the desert.

Overshadowed by the Pyramid of Khafre, a picnicking family watch indulgently as their youngest children share a sedate and closely supervised donkey ride.

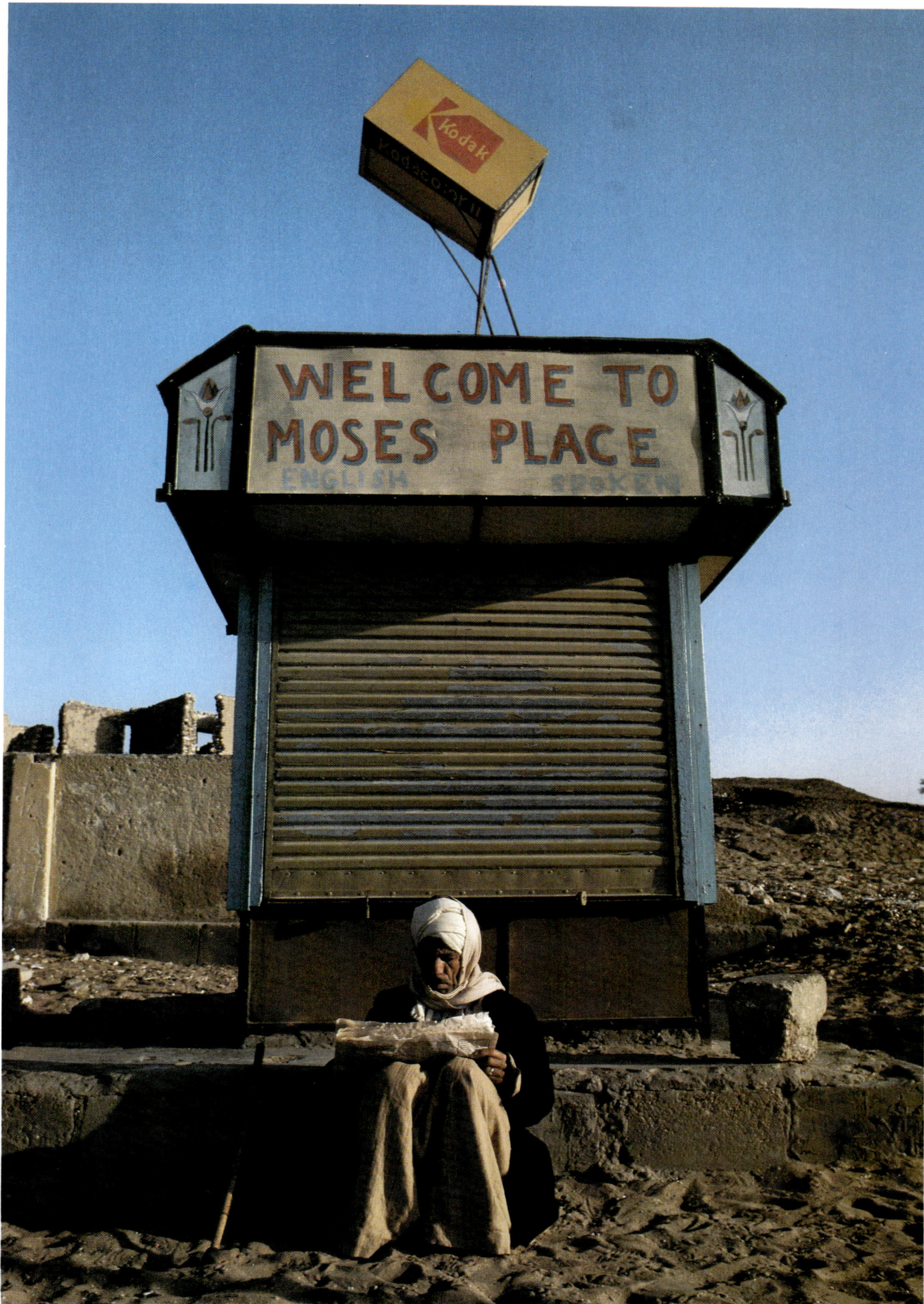

Before the arrival of the day's tourists, a guide peruses his newspaper beside a biblically named stall selling film for visitors' cameras.

A couple of Western travellers, just disgorged from a tourist coach, don Arab head-dress for the camera that will record their visit. Behind them, and partly obscured by the camel's head, the Sphinx commands the ceremonial approach to the Pyramid of Khafre (left). One theory holds that the lion-bodied Sphinx's features represented those of the Pharaoh himself.

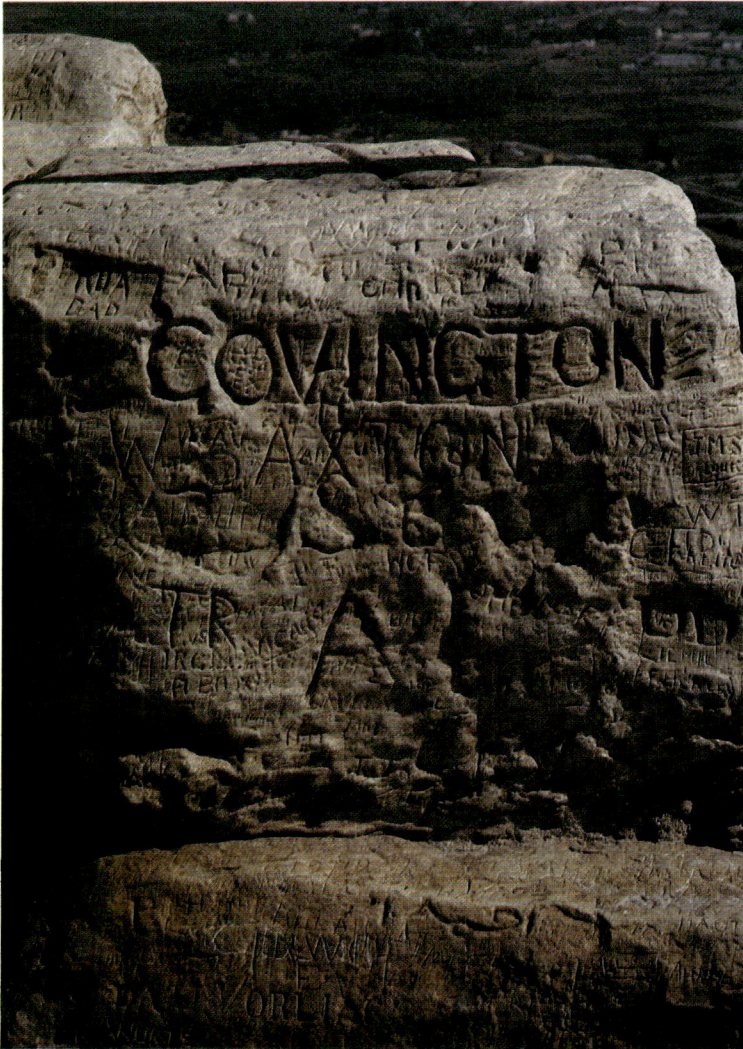

Names cut at the top of Khufu's Pyramid attest to generations of sightseers.

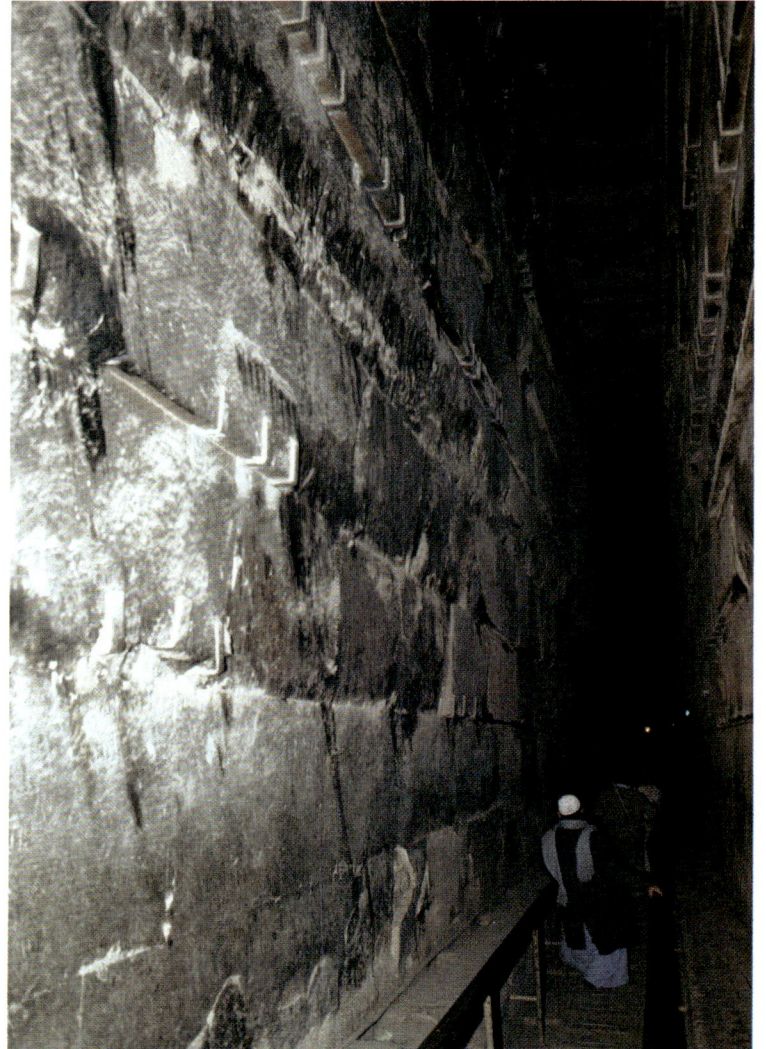

Inside the Pyramid, visitors file through the 153-foot-long Grand Gallery.

En route to the summit, boys climb up Khufu's weathered limestone blocks, exposed since the removal of the Pyramid's polished façade in the Middle Ages.

A chalet-style bungalow on a barren knoll provides its owners with a dramatic prospect of the three great Pyramids. Originally built in the 1930s as a base and storehouse for a party of German archaeologists, the house sports painted trompe-l'œil windows on the side that faces towards the blazing desert sun.

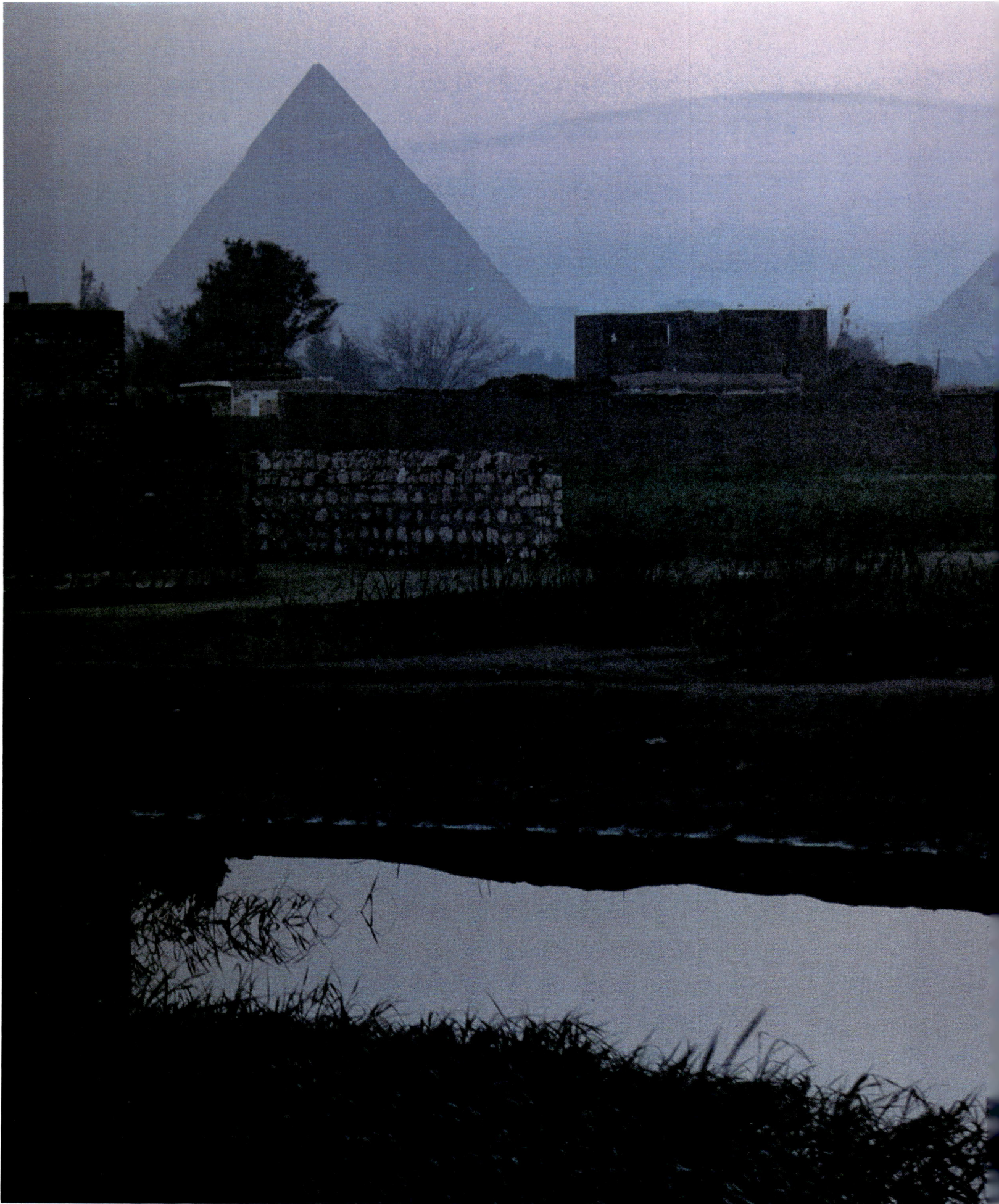

In a timeless scene, a farmer leads his camel and donkey along an irrigation canal as the pale light of dawn throws the Pyramids into ghostly relief.

5

Cross-Currents: Tradition and Change

To fathom present-day Cairene society one must appreciate fully the social as well as political importance of the Revolution of 1952 and the goals of its leader, Gamal Abdel Nasser. The son of a village postman from Bani Murr in Upper Egypt, Nasser had something of the typical southerner's passionate, intolerant character, which contrasts strongly with the easy-going nature of the Lower Egyptians, epitomized by Nasser's fellow officer and successor as President, Anwar Sadat.

Nasser responded to the cause of Egyptian nationalism from the age of 13, when he began to participate in anti-British demonstrations. He later studied at the Cairo Military Academy—not because he was particularly attracted to army life, his biographers claim, but because it offered an effective avenue for nationalist agitation. As a young officer of 30, Nasser fought bravely in the 1948 Arab-Israeli war and was wounded in a fierce rear-guard action near Gaza. The defeat of the Egyptian army was partly due to its inadequate weapons—outdated and sometimes defective, it was rumoured, because of racketeering by ministers close to the King. Nasser became convinced that Egypt would never regain its integrity and independence until the whole rotten fabric of the existing society had been purged and reconstituted. Four years after the war his underground group, the Free Officers, seized power in a military coup so skilfully organized that it succeeded virtually without bloodshed.

For Egypt, Nasser was the agent of the 20th Century, just as Muhammad 'Ali and the Khedive Isma'il had been agents of the 19th Century. Where they had allowed an élite of landowning royalists and foreign interests to dominate the country and monopolize its agricultural wealth, Nasser insisted that industrialization, modernization and an egalitarian nationalism were the only ways to regain independence and social justice. Big estates were confiscated and the land redistributed among former tenants. The maximum individual landholding was limited to 200 and later to one hundred feddans (a feddan is a fraction more than an acre). Industries and banking were nationalized. Factories were built by the government and an organized work-force was created: in 1952 only about 120,000 workers belonged to labour unions; by 1970 the figure had reached 3.2 million.

But Nasser's industrial achievements were less impressive than his social reforms. Between 1950 and 1971 the number of trained doctors in Egypt rose from 4,800 to 18,000 and, in spite of the upsurge in population, there was a noticeable improvement in health standards, reflected in the rise of average life expectancy from 42 to 53 years. Education received a

Clad in shimmering gilded costumes, girls of Mahmoud Ridah's troupe, Cairo's foremost folk-dance company, rehearse a routine derived from a court dance of Ottoman times. In the 1950s, Ridah was the first Egyptian to revive national dance forms, sometimes with modern refinements. Here, the dancers wear supporting helmets to eliminate the need for traditional balancing skills that would take years to learn.

similar investment; at one time the regime was opening local schools at the rate of two every three days. The number of students in higher education rose from a mere 75,000 in 1952 to almost one million in 1970.

From 1952 until his death in 1970, this large, powerfully built man ruled Egypt. His slow, rather formal gestures and his sheer physical presence recalled—consciously for some and unconsciously, probably, for many more—the colossal statues of the ancient Pharaohs. In any case, the Egyptian masses gave Nasser their adulation. He "belonged" to the Egyptian people in a way that no other ruler had done since the fall of the pharaonic kingdom to Persian invaders in the 6th Century B.C. His relationship with the people transcended mere politics: in his speeches—delivered in a voice that could be harsh and imperious, or velvety and seductive—he dramatized their aspirations and articulated their desire for personal dignity, suppressed by the centuries of foreign oppression. A new sense of national pride and identity was shared by all levels of society.

The most massive and spontaneous demonstration of Nasser's charisma came with his sudden death in September 1970 at the early age of 52. No one who was in Cairo at the time will ever forget those scenes. The Arab world was being racked with dissension over the civil war in Jordan, where King Hussein had unleashed his army against the Palestinians, who were using his country as a base from which to carry out guerrilla raids against the Israelis. Although seriously ill with diabetes and a heart condition, Nasser had worked tirelessly to achieve a reconciliation between Hussein and the Palestinian leader, Yassir Arafat. Just as his efforts had been crowned with success—when the Arab heads of state concerned, after an anguished conference in Cairo, finally reached agreement—Nasser suffered a massive heart attack. His doctors could not save him.

It was nightfall when Anwar Sadat, Egypt's Vice-President, announced Nasser's death on radio and television. The people of Cairo spontaneously surged into the streets and made their way to the government broadcasting station in Bulaq, as if driven to prove that the news was really untrue, that it was some cruel hallucination disseminated through the air-waves. Within hours, the streets around Bulaq were completely jammed and the cry rose all over the city: "The Lion is dead! The Lion is dead!" From towns and villages throughout Egypt, people began pouring into Cairo. By the morning of the funeral—which, contrary to Muslim custom, had to be delayed two days in order to allow foreign dignitaries to arrive—the city's population had swollen from four to eight million.

The authorities had planned a military funeral, accompanied by the well-ordered pomp and circumstance beloved of the martial mind. But the people would have none of it: Nasser was theirs and they were determined to reclaim him. Five divisions of infantry were not enough to keep them behind their cordons. As the procession set off from Gezirah, where the Free Officers had made their first headquarters, the people

Borne on a gun-carriage drawn by six black horses, the coffin of President Gamal Abdel Nasser is escorted by ranks of servicemen across Cairo on October 1, 1970, amid tumultuous scenes of mass grief. Nasser—architect of the 1952 nationalist Revolution and Egypt's President from 1956 until his death—attracted intense devotion from his countrymen, many of whom saw him as the greatest Egyptian leader since the Pharaohs.

surged forward. The heads of state and other visiting dignitaries were forced to abandon their positions at the head of the procession of mourners. Five thousand slow-stepping soldiers in ranks of 20 were barely able to push back the crowd at the Qasr al-Nil bridge. The progress amid the crowd of the flag-draped catafalque, mounted on a gun-carriage drawn by six black horses, resembled the passage of a ship through water when filmed in slow motion. The surging throng would momentarily part and close again in a swirling, bubbling wake. And all the while came the rhythmic chants of "Nasser! Nasser!" and "You live, eternal father!"

The changes wrought during Nasser's rule left Cairo a different city; yet, in a society with 5,000 years of recorded history, transformations cannot be total. New ideas must take effect by subtle assimilation into the existing fabric of life. The rationalist may find that this gradual process results in a mass of contradictions and confusions; but if he wants to understand the collision of tradition and change in Cairo, he is best advised to hold his preconceptions in check and simply observe how people behave.

A newcomer to Cairo, arriving in the city centre at about 11 o'clock on a Thursday night, might be excused for thinking that nine tenths of the city's population was male. It is the end of the working week—the "big night out" in the Egyptian capital; Friday, always the day of prayer, is in addition becoming more and more a day of rest. The busiest streets— those around neon-lit Tahrir Square or the dusty palm trees of Azbakiyah Gardens—are jammed with thousands of pedestrians—debouching from cinemas, crowded into cafés and restaurants, or simply strolling along the pavements, gazing idly at the goods in the shop windows. The over-whelming majority are male, mostly young, wearing shirts and trousers in the latest Western fashion, and often walking arm in arm. Very few women are to be seen and, of those, virtually none is alone. The scene will not surprise anyone familiar with the ways of Muslim countries, where women are invariably subject to some degree of social restriction. But in Cairo, simply because it resembles a European capital in so many respects, the absence of women seems remarkable and even anomalous.

In the Muslim world, Egyptian women have been in the vanguard of 20th-Century female emancipation, perhaps because Egypt—and par-ticularly Cairo—has long had Westerners, with their freer lifestyles, living there. In 1920, a celebrated suffragette and women's rights agitator, Huda Sharawi, set the example of discarding the veil that had customarily con-cealed the faces of women for centuries; she was soon followed by other women and by the 1940s the veil had almost completely disappeared. In 1956, four years after the Revolution, Egyptian women were among the first in the Muslim world to get the vote; and the National Charter of 1962, foundation-stone of the modern Egyptian state, asserts categorically that: "woman must be regarded equal to man, and she must . . . shed the

On the balding croquet lawn of the Gezirah Sporting Club, four casually dressed women players pursue a leisurely game in the late afternoon sun. Once the exclusive preserve of colonial foreigners, the club's 67 acres of sports facilities are now theoretically open to all; in practice, however, its clientele remains limited to the wealthy few who are able to afford the high annual subscription fees.

remaining shackles that impede her free movement so that she may play a constructive and profoundly important part in the shaping of the life of the country." Accordingly, the laws relating to the employment of women in Egypt are now as liberal as anywhere in the West; women are currently distinguishing themselves as members of the National Assembly, as doctors, lawyers, professors and architects—and even as airline pilots. The wives of immigrant fellahin often work in shops and factories.

But new laws cannot obliterate deeply rooted attitudes. Although women in Egypt are emancipated in many obvious ways, their position is, in practice, still largely governed by the prescriptions laid down 1,300 years ago in the Koran, which states: "Men have authority over women because God has made the one of them to excel the other, and because they spend their wealth to maintain them." For devout Egyptians of both sexes, therefore, the basically unequal status of men and women is considered to derive from the immutable word of God. Ten years after the Revolution, President Nasser stated that socialism, with its principle of individual equality, was not incompatible with Islam. Nevertheless, there remains a fundamental problem in reconciling the conflict between the State's dedication to the liberation of women and the teachings of the Koran.

The enshrinement of Koranic beliefs within the Egyptian legal system has meant that, in matters pertaining to the family, many major inequalities persist. For example, women still only inherit half as much of their parents' estate as their brothers. The Egyptian male is free to divorce his wife simply by publicly pronouncing the *talaq*—the words "I divorce thee"—three times, whereas the Egyptian woman may only divorce her husband if she has taken care to have a special "escape clause" written into the marriage contract, or can convince the civil courts that her husband is insane, cruel, impotent or unable to support her. She may have only one husband at a time, but he has the right to have up to four wives—a prerogative seldom exercised, however, chiefly because of the expense of paying the "bride-price" for each spouse and, later, of supporting her.

Marriage is not a private arrangement between individuals, but a legal contract between families. The contracting parties are invariably men: usually the groom and the bride's father. Women have little choice over whom they marry and sometimes are not even present at the signing of the contract.

On the other hand, an Egyptian woman who observes Muslim tradition enjoys many financial and social advantages. When she marries, her husband pays her a bride-price consisting of cash, jewellery, land or property—sometimes equivalent in value to several years of his income. Furthermore, Islamic law insists that the husband should support his wife and children, an obligation that remains even if the wife is financially independent. Indeed, under the "extended family" system, a man may find he has to support his wife's family as well as dependent relatives of his own. In the event of divorce, since the husband is not obliged to explain his decision, no social stigma is attached to the wife; she simply returns to live with her own family until such time as she may re-marry.

The full role of women can only be defined within the context of the family—still the corner-stone of all levels of Cairo's society. The strength of the Egyptian family lies in its solidarity. In addition to a husband, his wife and their unmarried children, each individual household may contain married sons—plus their wives and children—and perhaps a sister or mother who, having been widowed or divorced, has returned to the family fold. Intimate links are maintained as well with the households of the father's other relatives; for example, the children of poorer couples are often raised by more affluent members of the clan. The extended family of related households may sometimes total as many as a hundred people.

Because of the drift of country people into Cairo, many Egyptian families are physically dispersed. Yet, there is a constant interchange of visits. Country-dwellers often stay with relatives in Cairo in order to seek short-term employment or to take part in the *mulid* of their favourite saint; and city-dwellers will return to their ancestral village for family weddings or to help with the harvest. Thus, family solidarity is preserved, and, incidentally, the influence of the countryside upon the city maintained.

There is a clearly defined hierarchy in the Egyptian family. At the head of each unit is an all-powerful patriarch, who exercises absolute control over his family's finances, education and choice of marriage partners; he also dictates standards of personal conduct and religious observance. His relatives are expected to conform scrupulously to these standards, since any misdemeanour they may commit is held to reflect upon the family as

Seated on a ceremonial dais in the Nile Hilton Hotel, a popular social venue for wealthy Cairenes, a bride and bridegroom exchange confidences while their wedding guests are entertained by musicians. Such lavish functions, financed by the groom's family as a display of its wealth, are supplements to, and quite separate from, the civil ceremony, where the marriage contract is signed by the groom and a male relative of the bride—usually her father; the bride herself is often absent.

a whole. Thus, amongst traditionally minded Egyptians, an individual tends to be evaluated less on the strength of his own actions and achievements than upon the reputation of his family—a system that inevitably militates against individualism and social innovation. It is among educated urban families with factory or office jobs that the nearest approach to the Western nuclear family occurs, partly because independent employment makes it possible for sons to set up their own homes and families, instead of depending at least partly on the larger family unit for economic support.

Within the family, age dominates youth, and male usually takes precedence over female. According to the Koran, respect for one's parents is next in importance only to one's obligations towards God. Indeed, the deference shown by the young towards their elders is one of the most enduring features of Egyptian family life—and in some conservative households the father still expects his sons to greet him by kissing his hand.

Filial respect is, of course, strongest in families whose members have little contact with social and industrial organizations, such as colleges and factories, which exert their own influences on the younger generations. Family loyalty is no doubt reinforced by the widespread survival in Egypt of craft industries in which skills are handed down from father to son.

Egyptian children may respect their father, but they are closer to their mother, who plays the major role in their upbringing. Within the family women have a well-defined, if circumscribed, role. They have considerable influence, which increases with age. As mothers (or potential mothers) they are guardians of the family's future; by their scrupulously modest and correct behaviour, they are expected to safeguard its reputation. Their opinions weigh in the choice of a spouse—especially of wives for their sons. The Egyptian mother-in-law is a formidable figure and jokes about her are the stock-in-trade of many a comedian on radio and television.

But when it comes to claiming the equal place in the outside world to which the Constitution insists they are entitled, Cairene women find many difficulties in their way. Many upper-class girls attend a university—partly, no doubt, to improve their marriage prospects; a well-educated wife reflects favourably on a husband's status. If she earns money, it also makes a desirable addition to the family income. But throughout the Egyptian social scale, many husbands still consider it a point of honour to support their families single-handed; for them, a woman's primary duty is to look after her children at home. Muslim tradition, since it holds that a married woman may only work if it is absolutely essential to her family's finances, frowns upon her taking a job merely so as to afford "unnecessary" luxuries.

Acceptance of women who choose to exercise the skills their education has given them comes only slowly. I was once told an illuminating story about a woman who earned the post of chief engineer at a factory just outside Cairo. After a dogged struggle against the prejudices of her male subordinates, she eventually won their grudging respect for her professional brilliance. But they could not bring themselves to accept her as a woman; so they transformed her into an honorary man, and henceforth addressed her as "Mr. Engineer".

Even slower to be accepted is the idea of choice in sexual matters, especially for women. I remember watching an American television show in the company of a mixed group of sophisticated young Cairenes, all of them university graduates, in the prosperous suburb of Ma'adi. The episode concerned an unmarried girl who had rejected one lover—after spending the night with him—to return to her former sweetheart. Talking about the film afterwards, they focused, in a rather adolescent way, on the risqué elements—the kissing, cuddling, and so forth. When I sought to provoke discussion of the deeper element in the film—the question of *female* sexual choice—they seemed embarrassed and too genuinely disturbed to address the subject.

Behaviour between the sexes, even among the most modern young people, is usually very restrained. If they are adventurous, they may hold hands in public; if extremely daring, they may actually brave a kiss. But open signs of affection are exceptional. To the European, such formality contrasts oddly with the friendly intimacy between Egyptian men who hug, kiss, hold hands or link arms in a quite unaffected way. I remember that a dear friend once bade me farewell from Cairo by embracing me warmly, but his wife contented herself with a deliberate handshake.

Naturally, conflicts within families have grown more frequent and more painful as Western ideas have become more widely disseminated through

A Las Vegas-style neon sign glows in the night sky at the entrance to Sahara City, an open-air complex of nightclubs located just south of the Gizah Pyramids.

the numerous modern novels and films that are available in Cairo. Not many, however, have hastened to switch to the Western model of romantic freedom. "Love is only an emotion," says a character in a novel by Nagib Mahfuz, one of Egypt's most popular writers, "and you can cope with it one way or another; but marriage is an institution, a corporation not unlike the company I work for, with its own accepted laws and regulations. What's the good of going into it if it does not give one a push up the social ladder?" That remark demonstrates tellingly the resilience, amid all the changes of modern society, of the traditional view of marriage as a practical bargain between families, rather than as the expression of a romantic attraction between individuals.

The general acceptance of restraints on personal choice of a marriage partner, even among well-educated and liberal-minded Cairenes, was brought home to me as I attended a betrothal party held in the Nile Hilton. The young couple involved—Mustafa and Basman—had met at university. The legalities of the formal betrothal ceremony known as the *Katib al-kitabah* (the signing of the book) had been completed, and several hundred relatives and friends were gathered now for a great tribal celebration. Since Basman had not yet finished her studies, the actual marriage would be delayed for two years, at which time everyone would return to the Hilton for a pre-consummation feast on a similarly grand scale.

I asked Mustafa, a lecturer in medicine, to what extent he and Basman had been free to choose each other. "In my case," he said, "the choice was about 80 per cent free." And for Basman? He paused for thought, then replied, "In her case, about 10 per cent." And Basman, a bright-eyed girl, whom Mustafa claimed was the cleverest student in his class, demurely assented to this estimate.

The party itself was a compelling demonstration of the mixture of Egyptian and Western styles. As a family occasion *par excellence*, a betrothal or wedding is, for all classes in a Muslim community, one of the most lavishly celebrated. For many of the Europeanized bourgeoisie, grand hotels have become the obligatory venue.

"Display is the whole point of the thing," a member of the hotel's management pointed out to me. In this respect, today's Westernized bourgeoisie are being nothing if not traditional. In 19th-Century Cairo—according to the eyewitness account of the English scholar Edward Lane, who lived in the city in the 1820s and 1830s, before European influences had made significant inroads—the bride and the groom each took part in a separate procession through the streets on their wedding day, preceded by musicians and acrobats, and following a circuitous route so as to be seen by as many people as possible. The popularity of the Hilton among well-to-do modern Cairene couples is largely due to its cantilevered staircase, which rises dramatically from the foyer so that everyone can see the arrivals. The Hilton alone has about 400 such parties every

Undulating her voluptuous body, a tasselled entertainer—a 27-year-old sociology graduate—captivates her audience at Sahara City, a Cairo nightspot famous for its belly-dancers. Once the sole professional prerogative of one particular Egyptian tribe, performing as a belly-dancer can now be so lucrative that it attracts women of varied backgrounds.

year (it is not unusual to find more than one going on at the same time) and the hotel throws its own party once a year, broadcast on television, for all the couples who have celebrated their nuptials there.

At Basman and Mustafa's affair the guests were seated on arrival at small tables scattered across the Hilton's huge ballroom. Their fashions in dress varied dramatically. The men wore suits and ties; the older women, smart black gowns or billowing chiffons in pastel shades; and the young girls, pink or white dresses and flowers in their hair. However, among them could be seen old women wearing the traditional rural head-dress that resembles a white, knitted Balaclava helmet, thus revealing the recent origins of some branches of the family among the Egyptian peasantry. Since this was essentially a family occasion, the women were on their own ground and appeared to be very much in command, directing the proceedings efficiently. The men, temporarily pushed into the background, sat around looking awkward, or tried to make themselves useful by tinkering with movie-cameras and spotlights.

Suddenly there was a wail of bagpipes—an embellishment left over from British Army days—a thumping of drums and a rattling of tambourines. Everyone rushed outside to watch the betrothed couple making their ceremonial entrance from the foyer. They were preceded by the bagpipers and a dozen or so attendant girls bearing candles. Mustafa and Basman entered the ballroom—she in white, with floral bouquet, and he in velveteen tuxedo and frilly shirt. But the Western middle-class impression was soon dispelled: the teenage girls, until now so demure, raised the ancient cry of joy known as the *zagharit*, a shrill sound reminiscent of an American Indian war-whoop. The couple were escorted to a dais at one side of the room and there they sat for two hours, smiling bravely under the sweltering heat of the spotlights as an endless succession of guests— parents, in-laws, siblings, aunts, cousins, business associates and former schoolfellows—was brought forward to be photographed with them.

Meanwhile, the rest of us were served with cold meats, sandwiches, sweetmeats, jugs of fruit juice and pots of tea—no alcohol, for this was a Muslim feast—while entertainments were provided. A comedian delivered some jokes and mouthed imitations of musical instruments. He was followed by a belly-dancer, who gyrated her plump hips and ample bosom directly in front of the young couple. This struck me as surprising fare to set before two young people of such virginal demeanour; indeed, it was positively premature, since Mustafa and Basman—now holding hands in public for the first time—would not consummate their union for two years. Yet, equally, the explicit eroticism of the dance seemed appropriate to a Muslim culture where sexuality—within wedlock—is seen without disapproval, as an essential aspect of the duty of child-bearing.

Immediately after the belly-dancer there appeared a woman singer of traditional songs—gorgeous in blonde wig, long false eyelashes and a

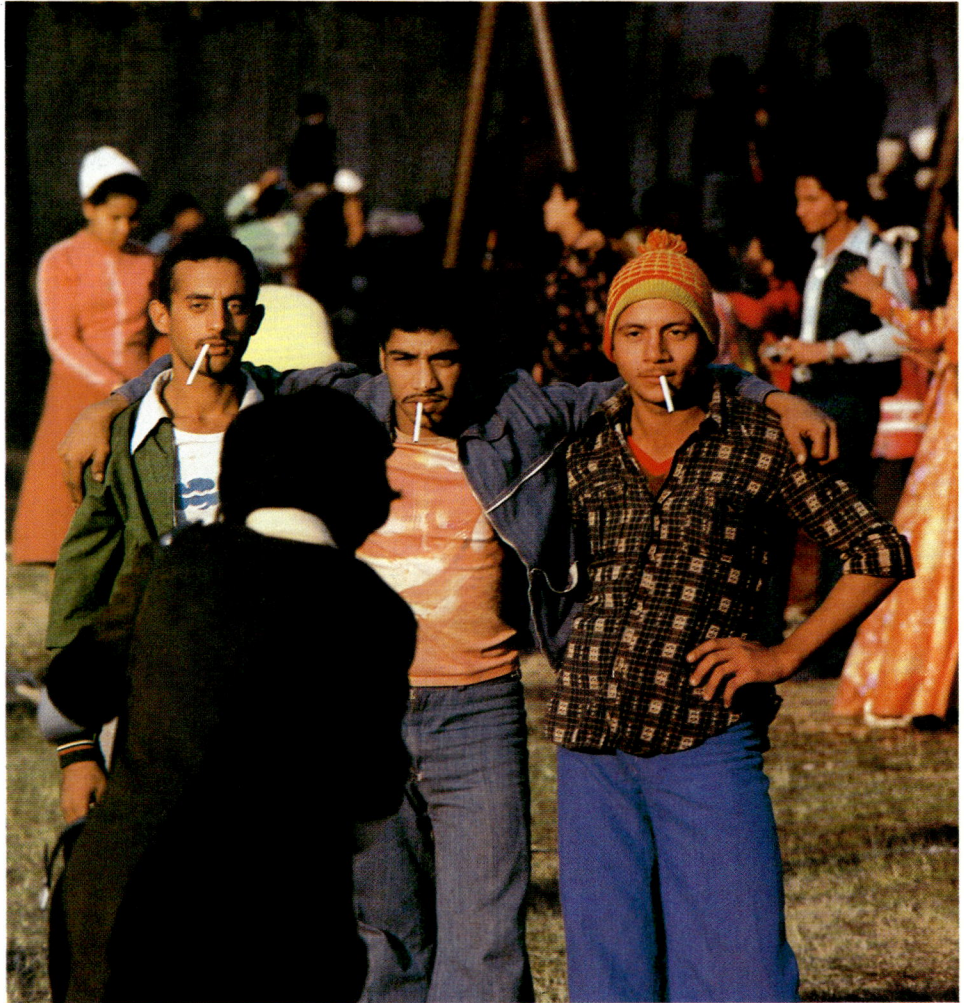

Strolling in Cairo's Zoological Gardens, three young men with unlit cigarettes strike studiedly masculine attitudes for a relative with a camera. The zoo, covering 21 acres on the Nile's west bank, is a favourite family haunt for outings— less for its collection of African animals than for the opportunity to play games, listen to music, dance and picnic under the trees.

crimson gown with plunging neckline. By now the party was in full swing. The assembled guests boisterously joined in the singing. A man removed his jacket, leapt on to the rostrum and partnered the singer in a vigorous folk-dance. Despite the absence of alcohol there was an atmosphere of uninhibited conviviality. At last, the grand climax came: after a solemn procession across the ballroom, Mustafa and Basman cut the cake—a five-tiered confection so tall that it could only be reached by means of a short step-ladder.

Pre-revolutionary Cairo was, of course, one of the most lavish pleasure centres of the Middle East; but Nasser's Revolution changed all that. Cairo was generally cleaned up, the brothels were closed and the belly-dancers were made to wear body-stockings to cover their midriffs. The pre-revolutionary élite disappeared en bloc, and in their place appeared a new upper class of powerful government officials, whose lifestyle was far less ostentatious than their predecessors'. Under the influence of the incorruptible and egalitarian Nasser, lavish displays of wealth became rare, and a regulation was introduced that restricted to £E5,000 ($7,500) a year the salary that any individual might openly receive—although, of course, "hidden" sources of income were less easily controlled, and innumerable ways round the restriction could be found.

Naturally, not quite all privilege was curtailed. The new élite lost little time, for example, in taking over exclusive institutions that the British had created, foremost among them being the Gezirah Sporting Club. Some

In the poor southern quarter of Sayyidah Zaynab, men and boys watch television in a local café. Many Cairenes have no television set, but almost all have access to programmes on state channels—if not at a nearby coffee-house, then at a community centre where a set is supplied by the government.

of the radicals among the Free Officers—including, reputedly, Nasser himself—wanted to close down the Gezirah Club as a symbol of imperial rule, in order to use its grounds for popular housing and a people's park. The Gezirah management cleverly outflanked them by extending membership—previously confined to the British and a few members of the old Turkish and Levantine élite—to Egyptian military officers and their families. By the time the government got round to considering closing the club, it discovered that its most influential political supporters had already become members. The plan was quietly dropped and, ever since, the Gezirah Club has been the haunt of fashionable Europeanized Egyptians. The horse-races held in winter on its oval track are always well attended.

For some, the post-Nasser society seemed a dark age of austerity—drab and dull; for others, it was the reaffirmation of proper values and national respectability. In any event, things changed again under Sadat, who relaxed controls on private enterprise and investment in an effort to stimulate the economy. To some extent, Cairo has taken the place of beleaguered Beirut as the main resort of pleasure for the Middle East, and after dark, nightclubs, cabarets and restaurants outline with their bright lights the Gizah road leading to the Pyramids.

Cairo continues to enjoy a thriving tourist industry, but Westerners who have come to see the Pyramids and the Sphinx are only a small—though growing—proportion of the visitors. More than half of each year's tourists are holiday-makers from oil-rich Arab countries where there are more austere Muslim traditions, who come to have a good time in Egypt's relaxed and sophisticated atmosphere. It is considered fashionable among Middle Eastern travellers to fly to Europe for holidays, but for those who speak only Arabic it is, of course, easier—as well as cheaper—to go to Cairo. Judging by their quips, the Cairenes often find the new visitors just as comical and arrogant as they found the Europeans in the old days.

The entertainment world that caters for tourists does, of course, attract some of Cairo's own inhabitants, particularly rich and fashionable younger males, but on the whole—as befits a society where the family has such paramount importance—leisure time is spent principally in family pursuits, such as the big picnics that mark the celebration of religious festivals, or an occasional evening out at a restaurant.

In general, all classes spend their money on conviviality rather than on possessions. The traditional Muslim home, even of an affluent family, is plainly furnished with cushions and carpets and simple Western-style tables and chairs. There are, however, plenty of Europeanized families who prefer all the trappings of a typical Western household. In many middle-class homes, for instance, it is still *de rigueur* to own the curious Middle Eastern and European hybrid furnishings known as "Luwis Khamastashar" (Louis XV), produced by dozens of joiners and cabinet-makers in the heart of Cairo around Bab al-Luq. Such heavily gilded and singularly uncomfortable French-style furniture first became fashionable in Ottoman times. It may have derived its popular name from the salon of the old Shepheard's Hotel, which was done in Louis XV style in the 1920s and represented the height of European sophistication at the time.

The preference for family outings and family occasions is just as strong among Cairenes who are less well off. Their cramped homes would, in any case, allow them little room for relaxation. One Friday afternoon, I visited the zoo in Gizah, located in one of the fine royal parks originally created by French landscape gardeners for the Khedive Isma'il. I found every available piece of its spacious grounds filled with people picnicking in intimate family groups under the stately palms and banyan trees, or amusing themselves with dancing and ball games. Few people were bothering to look at the animals, which do not thrive in confinement during the heat of a Cairene summer, and the atmosphere was relaxed and friendly. My wife and I were obviously the only foreigners there and many families made a point of offering us food or inviting us to join in their games.

A crowd had gathered by the old bandstand near the lake. In the old days a British military band, resplendent in red tunics trimmed with silver braid, would have played there, largely for the benefit of nannies wearing starched pinafores, and of their prettily dressed charges. Now it was the platform for a group of local musicians, who were joined by a young man with a skipping rope who performed an impromptu dance. His movements were those of a bantam cock, brimming with stylish, masculine vanity. But suddenly a sleek-looking man with silvery hair jumped up, pushed the previous performer out of the limelight and began his own dazzling dance. It lasted for several minutes and then, evidently pleased with the sensation he had created, he asked his rival to join him. Together they did a nimble *pas de deux*, while the crowd bubbled with glee. For me the occasion summed up perfectly the spontaneity and gregarious good humour of Cairo's people.

As you might expect in a community where the lives of men and women are so distinct, some forms of leisure activity are more or less exclusive to men and others to women.

Egyptian men, of course, have much greater social freedom than women. Although a good proportion of them are content to spend the evening at home with their families, others will go to sit for a few hours in the local village-style café. It is said that there are at least 6,000 of them in Cairo. These unpretentious institutions usually consist of a single room with colour-washed walls and a floor of beaten earth or concrete, furnished with a few wooden tables and chairs. Although soft drinks—and, very occasionally, beer—are available in such cafés, the most popular beverages are thick, black coffee, served in minute cups, and glasses of tea—both prepared by the proprietor over a small paraffin stove. In Egypt, tea comes

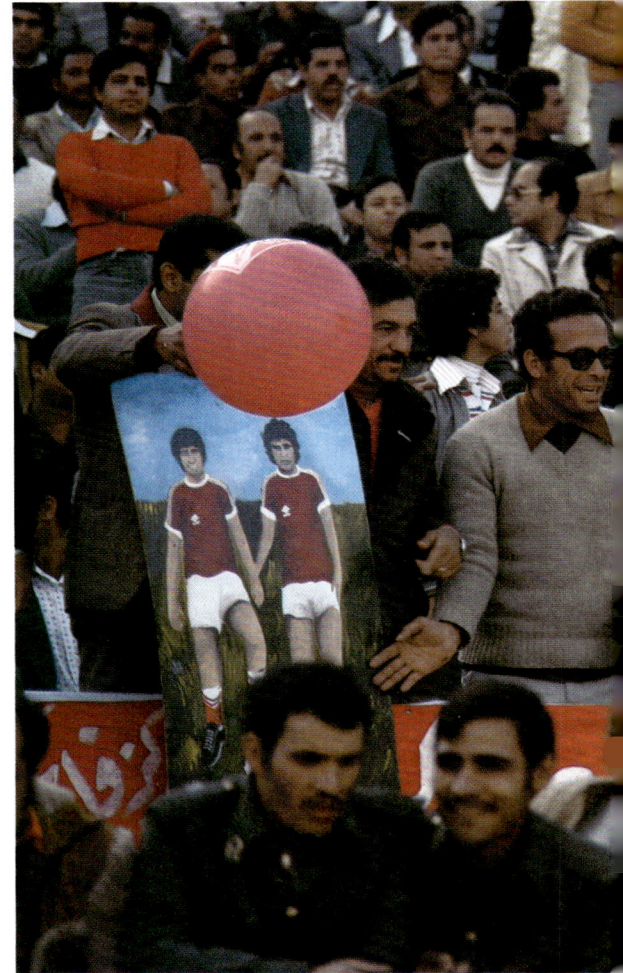

Fervent supporters proudly hold up portraits of their soccer idols before a kick-off between Ahli and Zamalik, Cairo's top professional teams. Soccer is by far the city's most popular sport; the 100,000-seat stadium at the satellite Nasr City is regularly packed for matches.

in many varieties: there is the black *sa'idi* ("southern-style"), brewed for hours and heavily sugared; the *fellaha* ("peasant-style"), marginally less strong and less sweet; and the *inglizi* ("English-style"), for which boiling water is simply poured over the tea-leaves. Customers lounge about at the tables, playing *tawlah* (backgammon) or *konkan* (an elaborate card-game), reading the newspapers placed at their disposal, or watching the television set in the corner of the room. A group of men will sometimes hire a *shishah* (water-pipe), and then pass it among themselves.

But the chief café amusement is conversation. Egyptians are constantly on the lookout for something new to talk about and the topics they choose range far beyond mere gossip, to politics and the more abstruse aspects of theology and science. A favourite sport, much enjoyed by everyone present, is for one man to tease his companion about some particularly sensitive issue until he explodes into rage, accompanied by much good-humoured shouting and waving of hands.

Another traditional place of relaxation for menfolk in Cairo is the hashish parlour, many of which survive—despite their official illegality—in the older districts of the city. In present-day Egypt, the use of hashish is in theory punishable by stiff legal penalties, and the more sober citizens view it with considerable disapproval; nevertheless hashish is plentifully available for those who know how to find it.

I have spent an evening in a Cairo hashish parlour. After reassuring themselves that I was in no way connected with the police, the customers told me that they bought hashish—a black resin—from a clandestine supplier "just round the corner" and brought it with them to the parlour, ostensibly a café that served only tea and coffee. I watched as an assistant prepared a trayful of "stones" or pipe-tops—small, mushroom-shaped stoppers of perforated earthenware—upon each of which he sprinkled flakes of resin. He then fitted one of the "stones" into the top of a special *shishah*—with a three-foot-long bamboo stem in place of the usual flexible hose—and ignited the resin with glowing charcoal that he carried in a small metal basket. As soon as each customer had smoked several "stones", drawing the smoke down through the cooling water in the body of the *shishah*, he passed the apparatus on to his neighbour.

In the past, hashish-smoking in Egypt was most prevalent among the poor, chiefly because it was cheap and plentiful, and provided welcome moments of relaxed euphoria amid the drudgery of peasant life. By contrast, alcohol was both expensive and, under Islamic law, illegal. Hashish is not explicitly condemned in the Koran, for the reason that its use was unknown in Arabia during the Prophet's time. When hashish eventually reached Egypt—from Persia during the 13th Century—the Muslim authorities, in the absence of a Koranic prohibition, found it difficult to legislate against its use. They fell back on the argument that the Koranic ban on "wine" is, by implication, a ban on intoxicants of all kinds.

But the hashish lobby successfully resisted its banning—at least until the arrival of the Europeans, who persuaded the Egyptian government to declare the drug illegal. Present-day devotees are well aware that hashish is forbidden both by Muslim tradition and the law (which is nonetheless widely evaded); they therefore use it discreetly, in quiet cafés or the seclusion of their homes, where they can enjoy its pleasantly relaxing effects—a sense of physical detachment and mental exhilaration. Since the 1952 Revolution, with its reorganization of the social structure, the habit of hashish-smoking has spread beyond peasant circles. In the hashish parlour I visited, conversation was flowing freely and democratically among a labourer in a blue *galabiyah*, a civil servant in a neat safari suit and—surprisingly—an army colonel in full uniform.

Unlike hashish, alcohol is openly on sale throughout Cairo. Much of it —especially wine and beer—is made in Egypt, although the National Assembly makes periodic attempts to ban its manufacture. Indeed, in spite of the fact that the more cosmopolitan Egyptians can often be seen drinking in the luxury hotels and Western-style bars of Cairo's city centre, there is a growing popular movement in favour of total prohibition, in accordance with Koranic strictures.

Most of the social life for women is conducted at home, and even today the larger traditional houses of Cairo often contain a distinct women's quarter, to which the ladies of the household invite their female friends for tea-parties and gossip, and from which adult males—other than close relatives and servants—are firmly excluded.

Among the liberated upper classes of Cairo, women are increasingly seeking their relaxations outside the home. But in less sophisticated sections of society, their chances of escaping from the family circle and mixing with other women are still limited. One of the few available opportunities is provided by a visit to a *zar*—an ancient ritual involving dance, music and incantation that is performed in order to exorcize a person thought to be possessed by an evil spirit. The *zar* (literally "visitation") was probably introduced into Egypt by Ethiopian slave women during the 18th Century, and its survival into modern times is evidence of the belief in magic and the supernatural that is still firmly held by many uneducated Egyptians. For most women, however, the *zar* is primarily a social occasion; they go along to watch rather than to take part.

The *zar* is based on the notion that many personal misfortunes—including physical and mental illness, marital problems, or simply a run of bad luck—are caused by *jinns* (spirits) that have taken possession of the victim and must be expelled—or at least appeased—if the misfortunes are to cease. A person so afflicted will consult the local *zar* practitioner, or sheikh, who for a small fee will diagnose the *jinn* that is causing the problem and ask it what the sufferer must do to obtain release. In mild

Surmounting one of the many nightclubs that line the road leading to the Gizah Pyramids, a concrete model of the Eiffel Tower promises entertainment of Parisian sophistication. With a strongly European flavour added to its more traditional repertoire, Cairo's cosmopolitan night-life is designed to appeal both to Western visitors and to the large number of wealthy tourists from neighbouring Arab countries.

cases, the required actions can include the wearing of a magic charm or a garment of a particular colour and the sacrificing of animals. In stubborn cases, the sheikh will recommend the holding of a *zar*, sometimes in private, at the patient's home, but more often in public, before a paying audience. Since most of the sheikh's customers are women, the ceremony frequently takes the form of a symbolic "marriage" between the patient and the *jinn*, who is thereby transformed into a powerful protecting spirit.

Although a *jinn* is quite likely to be held responsible for the entire range of problems—physical, mental and social—afflicting the person it has possessed, some of the spirits are associated with specific complaints. The names given to *jinns* often allude to this association: thus, Sultan Ahmar (the Red Sultan) is particularly notorious for causing haemorrhages and should be placated by, for instance, wearing a red cloak and burning red candles, both during the *zar* and at home. Al Sudani (The Sudanese)— so named in allusion to the volatile temperament that is allegedly characteristic of that nation's inhabitants—is considered to be the most violent of *jinns* and is therefore believed to cause, for example, marital quarrels and physical convulsions.

I once had the opportunity to witness a *zar*, held in a small brick store-room alongside the shabby tenements of the Ain al-Sirah housing estate, on the southern outskirts of Cairo. The floor was crowded with squatting women of all ages, from teenage girls in bright print dresses to toothless grandmothers. Doors and windows had been deliberately sealed in order to produce a hot, foetid atmosphere, for it is thought that *jinns* are more likely to jump from the body when it is sweating.

As I arrived with a female friend, we saw a lean-faced woman of about 50 taking off her cloak to reveal a white wedding-dress stretched tight over her everyday clothes, in preparation for her "marriage" to the *jinn*. Accompanied by the hypnotic music of a flute, a drum and a tambourine, she began to dance with an urgent rhythm, making suggestive thrusts with her hips. The woman, I later discovered, had a history of internal bleeding and therefore, while she danced, the sheikh intoned an appeal to the Red Sultan, the *jinn* thought to be possessing her:

> "Red king of kings, you king of jinns,
> Recall your spirits, that all of them may attend.
> O you little bride, holding a lighted candle in
>   your hand,
> You are the bride of the Sultan,
> And your bridegroom is like a lighted candle."

At last, the woman seemed to feel that her spirit "bridegroom", satisfied with her performance, had left her body; and at that point she collapsed into a state of dazed, perspiring exhaustion.

Next it was the turn of a dark-skinned adolescent, probably a Nubian, who removed her headscarf to reveal waist-length tresses of silky black hair which she tossed about wildly. Clearly her *jinn* was especially persistent (or perhaps, as I did, the spirit was enjoying the performance), for the abandoned dance went on for what seemed like an hour. Only when the sheikh himself intervened by stopping the music was the dancer finally prevailed upon to resume her place among the waiting patients.

And so the rituals continued for the best part of a day. At intervals the woman who had organized the *zar* on behalf of the sheikh asked the spectators for money, beckoning them with a pair of small brass hand-cymbals that she clashed to the beat of the drum. The sums required were often the equivalent of half the daily wage of a labourer, but we foreigners had to pay much more for the privilege of watching. Once relieved of our money, we were unceremoniously requested to leave.

The *zar* is strongly condemned by Muslim authorities, and ordinary Egyptians dismiss it as a weakness of credulous housewives who have nothing better to do. Most women, it seems, attend without their husband's knowledge. Yet, medical authorities have claimed that the experience of dancing at a *zar* can be beneficial for women suffering from ailments with psychosomatic origins; as in the group psychotherapy practised in the West, the patient derives support from the other people present. The spectators are obviously less involved, but enjoy the *zar* as a social occasion; one girl in the audience admitted to the woman who had taken me along that she did not believe in *jinns*, but had come because she liked the music and the chance to be among other women.

One of the most significant influences upon the whole of Egyptian society has been that of modern broadcasting, still largely a monopoly of the State. The most spectacular modern building in Cairo, ordained by Nasser as both a symbol of his regime's methods and a monument to its special taste, is the huge broadcasting station on the banks of the Nile at Bulaq; the vast circular edifice, topped by a square office tower that appears to bear no relation to it, contains 43 radio and 11 television studios, and accommodates a programme and engineering staff of some 10,000—more people than are employed in broadcasting by all the other Arab and African countries combined.

Nasser's Revolution coincided with the development of the transistor radio. Arabic, with its rich inflections and powerful range of imagery, is made for broadcasting; and at least one in six Egyptians owns a radio. Furthermore, the Arabs, as I have said, are a people who are especially sensitive to singing, poetry and recitation. Egypt has four domestic radio networks that, in addition to news and popular entertainment, offer religious broadcasts, European-language programmes and items of special interest to farmers, factory workers and the armed forces. The state-run television service, inaugurated in 1961, was the first in Africa. Of its two channels, the principal one can be received all over Egypt, but the

Sitting among visitors as well as other "patients", a woman falls into a trance while taking part in a zar: a folk ceremony for females that purports to banish malevolent jinns, or spirits. In Cairo, such occasions—part superstitious ritual, part group therapy—are held regularly and attended by women seeking cures for ills arising from psychological stress, or simply an escape from domestic routine.

other is restricted to Cairo and Alexandria, where most of the nation's television sets are concentrated.

Once a nerve-centre for revolutionary Arab nationalism, the Egyptian broadcasting system under Sadat lost much of its early political fervour. What the Egyptians want is entertainment. As befits a nation composed largely of down-to-earth peasants, tastes are hardly sophisticated. Not for them the gloomy verbose plays, the earnest documentaries, and the cosy domestic soap operas of Western television. The Egyptians prefer the maximum of laughter and action, and the minimum of dialogue: the only conversations they enjoy are the ones they can take part in. Their favourite programmes are therefore farces starring knockabout comedians, police dramas involving at least one car chase and a shoot-out—and, of course, variety spectaculars starring folk singers and dancers.

Despite its preoccupation with none-too-demanding entertainment, Egyptian television does not escape the sterner influence of Islam. Throughout the day, at the times ordained by the Koran for private prayer, programmes are suddenly halted and a message is flashed on the screen to remind viewers of their religious duty. The showing of a Western-made documentary film on science or natural history is often followed by a studio discussion between Muslim scholars, who explain to viewers how the ideas within the film can be reconciled with orthodox Islamic thought.

In some ways, the most striking manifestation of the "global village" that has been created by television is the popularity in Egypt of soccer. When television arrived, the Egyptians became a nation of soccer addicts almost overnight. Most Cairenes had barely encountered the sport before seeing matches on the television screen, but now boys no older than three will create an impromptu game on any piece of empty ground. The huge new stadium at Nasr City, which has a capacity of 100,000—comparable to London's Wembley Stadium—is regularly filled for the important matches that are held at least once a week during the soccer season.

On the day of the World Cup semi-final between Holland and Italy in 1978, I happened to fall into conversation in the street with a friendly young Egyptian. It turned out that he was anxious to watch the match at the home of some distant relatives. "I'll tell them you're from Holland," he said, "and desperate to see your team play. Don't worry, you can pretend you don't speak Arabic." Before I could protest I was rushed up an unlit, rubbish-strewn staircase and ushered into a tiny kitchen, where at least 15 people, from grandmother down to the newest child, were ranged around the flickering set. On hearing I was from Holland, they were awe-struck at their good fortune, backing "my" team with feverish enthusiasm. I was seated in the place of honour and plied with offerings of tea, coffee and cakes. As the Dutch team's fortunes declined and finally collapsed, a gloomy silence descended on the company. I was treated with the solicitude usually reserved for one who has suffered a death in the family.

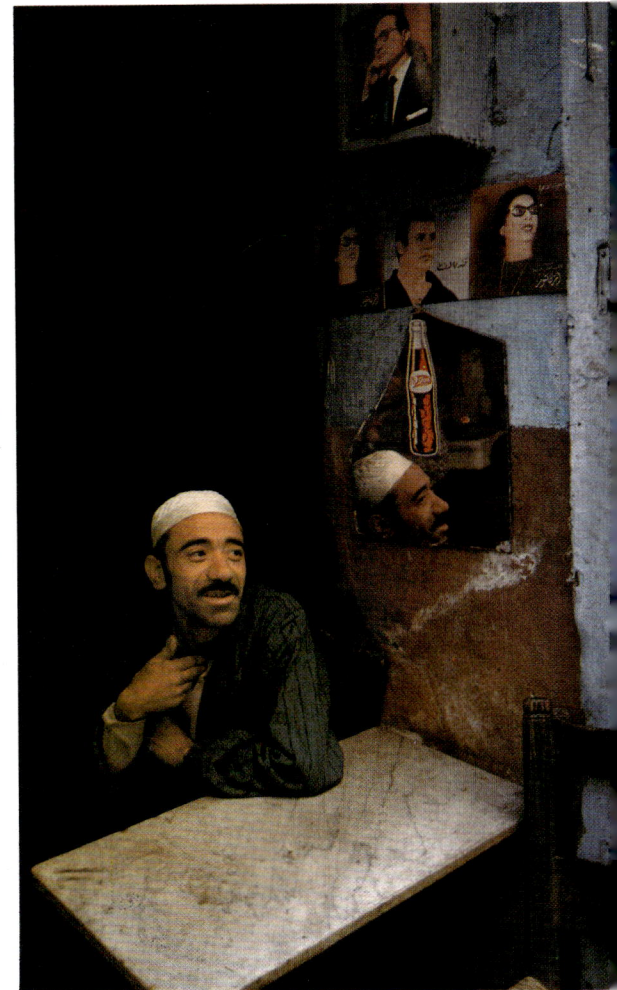

Reflected in the broken mirror adorning a back-street café, the image of a Cairene joins a gallery of popular Egyptian singers. The two identical photographs, originally used as record covers, testify to the unchallengeable supremacy of the greatest Arab woman singer of all: the immortal Umm Kulthum, whose immensely powerful, yet controlled, voice, and emotional delivery, brought her a following that continued to idolize her long after her death in 1975.

"God will bring you better luck next time, Insha' Allah [God willing]," they said, as I departed, slightly ashamed at the deception.

Among the musicians who broadcast on Cairo's radio and television, Egypt has its share of rock singers, who usually purvey Arabic "cover versions" of Western hits. But most of the population prefer to hear broadcast songs in the folk tradition that reflect more closely their own day-to-day experience. Indeed, probably the only person to rival Nasser in her charismatic hold over the masses was Umm Kulthum, Egypt's greatest woman singer of recent years. If Nasser was Egypt's father-figure, then Umm Kulthum was undoubtedly its mother-figure. Her songs, carried over the air-waves, were heard throughout the Arab world and brought vivid meaning to the sense of unity that Nasser tried to foster as a statesman.

A large, strongly built woman of peasant stock, she began her musical career in the traditional way, by reciting the Koran at village weddings and other rural gatherings. But soon her exceptionally beautiful voice—as powerful as that of any Western opera singer—made her a star all over Egypt. As was fitting in a society of arranged marriages, she sang not of the joys of love but of the pangs of unrequited passion, bringing tears to the eyes of even hard-faced army officers. In songs such as *"Khuf Allah"* ("Fear of God"), she expressed the deep religious convictions of the Egyptian people. Everything about Umm Kulthum was prodigious. She was able to sustain a single note for a minute and a half. Her concerts lasted five hours or more; one of her best-known songs, *"Anta 'Umri"* ("You are my life"), with its endless, mesmerizing melodic variations, frequently went on for two and a half hours. It is said that Nasser would never make a major speech on a night when one of her performances was being broadcast on another channel, for fear of the competition.

When Umm Kulthum died in February 1975, at the age of about 77 (although no one knew exactly), the scenes witnessed at Nasser's funeral less than five years earlier were duplicated. Once again, the people of Egypt flocked into Cairo to demonstrate their grief and their adulation. Once again, the police cordons in the city centre collapsed against the weight of the crowds struggling to touch or kiss their idol's coffin. So great was the throng of mourners, waving their handkerchiefs to the rhythmic chanting of "Farewell, Beloved Lyre!", that the squad of firemen carrying the coffin had to place it in an ambulance. They carried Umm Kulthum to the tomb that she had prepared for herself—as befitted a popular queen—in the ancient Eastern Cemetery under the Muqattam Hills.

Getting from Here to There

A Cairene carter urges his horse into a brisk trot, out-pacing a more leisurely colleague. The high-wheeled design of the carts has been current for centuries.

Cairo's traffic is an incongruous mixture in which ancient and modern transport meet on equal terms. In the last few years of the 1970s the number of automobiles in Cairo leapt more than three-fold; but the city's archaic street layout remains adequate only for a non-motorized age. The result has been chaos, in which vehicles are brought to a jammed, hooting stop at every major road junction. The public transport system seldom has sufficient buses and trains to cope with demand, and many passengers travel clinging on the outside—to doors, windows and each other. In such conditions, donkeys, horses, camels and mules still have advantages over mechanical transport: they are cheaper to operate, just as fast in thick traffic, and often more reliable. It is not unusual to see a draught animal towing away a mechanized casualty in the drama of a city on the move.

Agile commuters use windows to seek access to a bus already crammed with rush-hour passengers.

A swarm of rail travellers gain a precarious foothold on a locomotive. Lying flat on the train's roof, another passenger shades his eyes against the sun.

Putting his cart to use as a taxi, a peasant from an outlying village with no bus service brings local women and children into Cairo for a day's marketing.

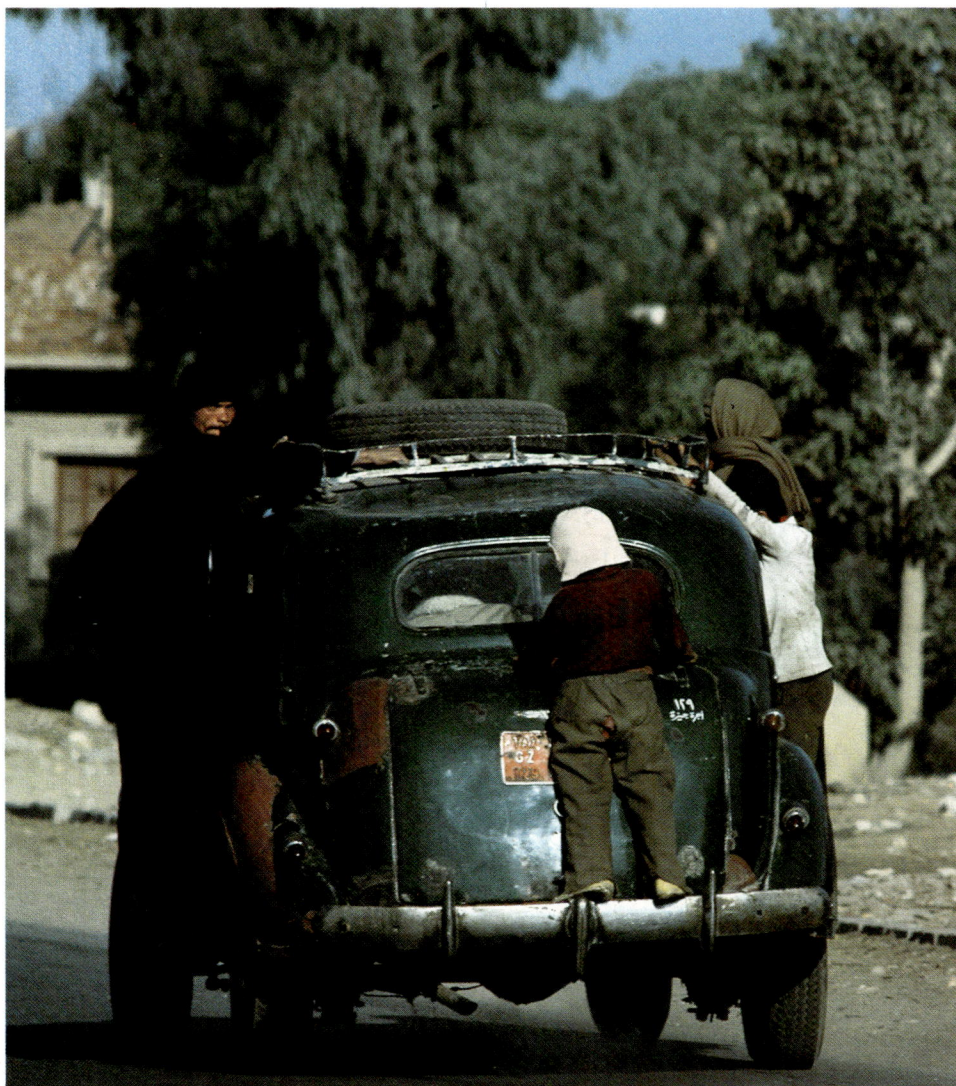

Already full up inside, a venerable cab transports supernumerary passengers on its running-boards.

Commuters on an overloaded ferry plying between the southern suburb of Ma'adi and the Nile's west bank crowd towards the bow as the vessel approaches land.

A hawker's makeshift vehicle—a cart propelled by a bicycle attached to its rear—serves as a stall for his multifarious stock of automobile spare parts.

On the city's rural fringe, a donkey plods along under a load of sugar-cane.

Slow but dependable, a mule tows a broken-down automobile, already much repaired, on a cart.

عين الناس غداره و عين الله

MAZDA

Wearing aloof expressions, two newly purchased camels are taken home. As they have done for centuries, camels still serve Egypt as efficient freight-carriers.

6

A Future in the Balance

Whatever your feelings for Cairo, you cannot escape the impression that it is a city on the verge of complete breakdown. Portents of an urban doomsday are apparent everywhere—most conspicuously in the city's decrepit public services and amenities. Public transport is woefully inadequate. Yet the roads cannot cope with the level of traffic and are often choked with blaring, fuming automobiles. Power cuts occur with infuriating regularity. Pipes in the sewage system frequently burst, turning some sections of road into foul morasses and posing a health hazard. When I was working in Cairo, telephones operated only intermittently; I sometimes had to dial 15 times and more to obtain a local number, and international calls were sometimes delayed for two or three days. I even heard tales of foreign businessmen who would make the hour-long flight to Athens to place an important call. Water pressure is frequently so low that household taps in upper storeys often produce nothing more than a trickle of rusty liquid to the accompaniment of a mocking gurgle. Parts of the city are sometimes without water for days at a time.

Chronic overpopulation and lack of modernization are the root causes of all these ills. Since the turn of the century, Cairo's population has soared from 600,000 to some nine million, with no corresponding development in municipal services. These remain substantially at the level they had reached in the 1920s, when they were intended to serve a city of, at most, three million. The notorious sewage system, for example, was completed in 1920 and has been extended only minimally since then. In 1967, a long-heralded disaster finally occurred when the system overflowed throughout Cairo; but much of the underlying inadequacy has gone unremedied. The water supply is of similar antiquity. The master plans for both systems (if they ever existed) have been lost; the result is long delays in carrying out repairs whenever the systems break down at any point, while exploratory excavations are made to try to locate the trouble.

The city's population continues to rise by about 4.5 per cent annually, due partly to Cairo's high birth rate (one of the highest in the world) and partly to the constant influx of fellahin who are attracted by the prospect of jobs at the steel and iron works, chemical plants and textile factories that have sprung up around the capital since the 1952 Revolution. The newcomers are also drawn by Cairo's educational and health facilities, and by the future opportunities that the city affords their children; but these programmes, too, are seriously over-extended. The rural immigrants also exacerbate Cairo's already severe housing shortage: in the old port of

An aerial view of the medieval al-Ghawriyah quarter emphasizes the value of rooftop space in the chronically overpopulated city. Citizens count themselves especially fortunate if they have access to a roof where—according to the customs of rural life—they can dry washing, relax in the cool of the evening and perhaps erect a wooden shack as an extra room.

Bulaq, for example, an area of two-to-four-storey houses, the population density is greater than in high-rise areas of New York and Tokyo.

To add to this catalogue of woes, Egypt's long-range attempts to expand its economy have been badly affected by the economic reverses arising from its conflicts with Israel. In Cairo, many foods are sometimes scarce and expensive, even such traditionally cheap and plentiful native fare as fish and fruit, although the government prides itself on guaranteeing that bread is available at half a piastre a loaf (about 1 cent). Less than 4 per cent of Egypt's 386,900-square-mile territory is cultivable—much of which is used to grow cotton for export—and the tiny proportion remaining is insufficient to produce all the food required by the population. Meanwhile, prices of imported foods steadily rise and, although the government attempts to shield the population with food subsidies provided through government shops and ration cards, its efforts are necessarily limited by the other heavy demands on its resources. To complete the vicious circle, even the meagre proportion of Egyptian agricultural land is being steadily sacrificed as the built-up area of the city inexorably spreads over neighbouring farmland to accommodate the spiralling population.

"Cairo is in the process of self-strangulation," a civil servant told me, "and we don't have the resources to save it." His gloomy opinion is hard to quarrel with; yet I myself do not share it. Cairo has been close to the breaking point ever since the Revolution; but against all the odds it has survived each crisis in turn and I am optimistic that it will weather its present difficulties too.

Not all the government's experts are as pessimistic as the one just quoted. Many of the optimists point to the benefits that have accrued from the economic reforms that were introduced after Egypt's 1973 war with Israel. Since Egypt lacked the finances for reconstruction, President Sadat introduced his so-called "open door" policy to attract foreign investors and break the shackles that constrained the socialist economy during Nasser's austere era of reorganization and nationalization. Although large-scale private and foreign investment failed to materialize in the first five years of the policy, some parts of Cairo benefited by the setting up of various building projects, such as hotels, office blocks and apartments, undertaken by a variety of foreign construction companies. And since foreign investors were reluctant to commit money to a city plagued with communications problems and inadequate public services, the Cairo authorities were forced to address the long-overdue task of overhauling or replacing the city's sewage, telephone, water and public transport systems.

In time, the optimists argue, the people of Cairo as a whole will benefit from these improvements. My own grounds for optimism about Cairo's future are less tangible: I believe, quite simply, that the Cairenes themselves have a resilience and an ingenuity that will enable them to contend with the vicissitudes of their city's painful development. When I expressed

Building workers form a human chain to lift wooden scaffolding planks to the top of an apartment block being built on the Nile's west bank. Under pressure from the city's exploding population, thousands of acres of rich agricultural land on the west bank have been swallowed up by building developments since the 1960s—a process the government tries to check by creating residential satellite cities in otherwise unproductive desert areas.

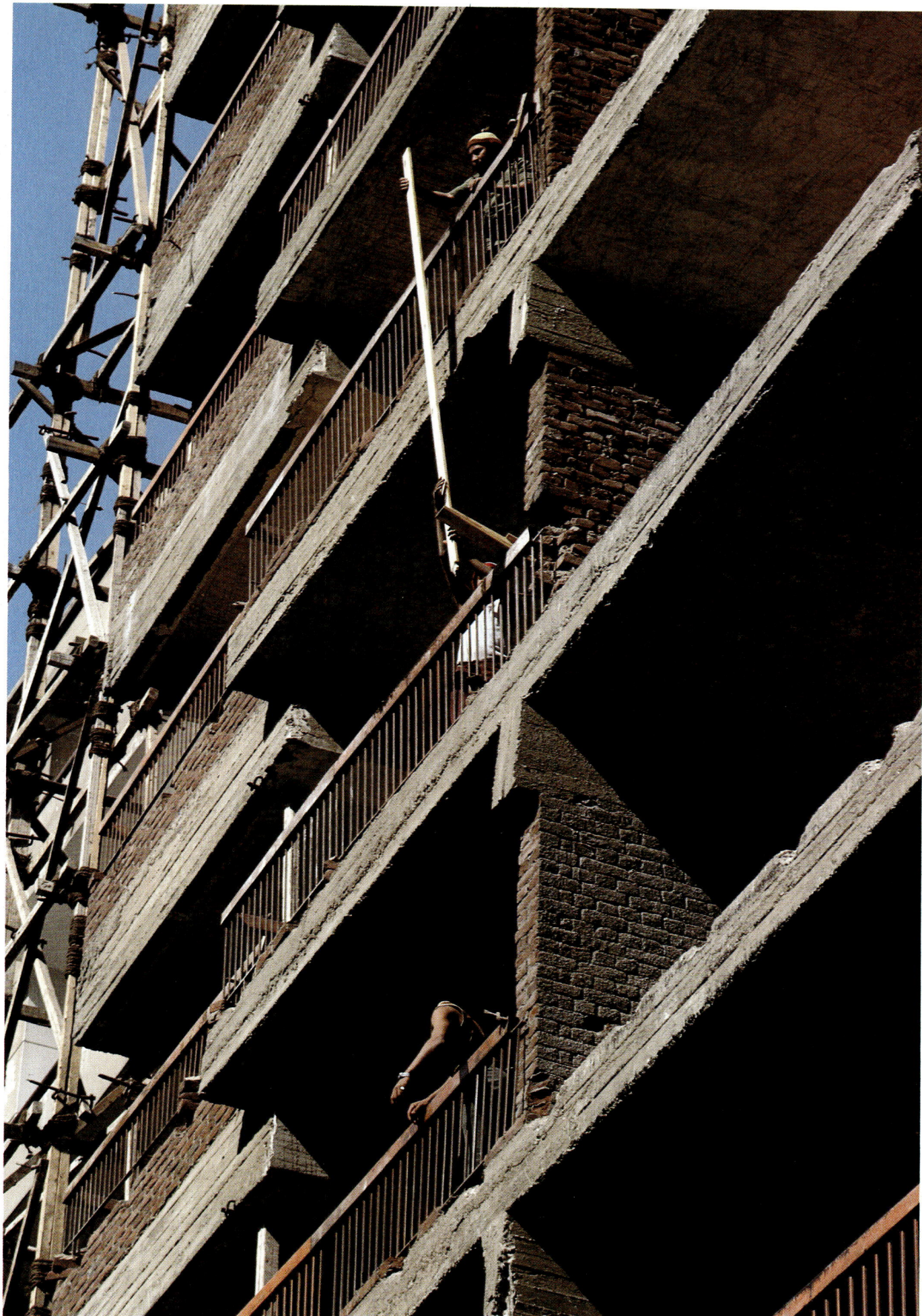

this opinion to an American oilman who was doing business in Cairo, he was sceptical. Having been frustrated by dealing with officials who had consistently failed to keep appointments or who stranded him in a bureaucratic quagmire, he was convinced that every worker in the city was hopelessly inefficient or corrupt. "All right," he demanded. "If they're so damned clever, then why the hell doesn't anything work?" The answer is that Cairo *does* work; but it works strictly on its own terms.

In fairness to the oilman, I hasten to add that Cairo works not through any strokes of genius on the part of its administrators. Quite the reverse, for Cairo's public agencies are arguably a major source of the capital's ills. Registered government officials in the civil service and public sector companies now make up almost a quarter of Cairo's entire working population; this overblown bureaucracy constitutes a gargantuan parasite feeding off Egyptian society. Decisions are delayed for months, years, decades. Businessmen, who have dubbed the national economic plan the "door ajar" policy, complain that even after their projects are approved by the highest authorities, they still have to tackle more than a dozen different agencies to see their plans through. Corruption is endemic, since officials are often so inadequately paid that they tend to regard bribes as the legitimate perquisites of office—as do most of those who offer the bribes.

A large complement of bureaucrats is to be expected in a city that is not only the capital of the nation but also the seat of a provincial government and the centre of industry and commerce. But Cairo's roles provide only a partial explanation for the number of its public employees. In fact, since the 1960s, the Egyptian government has automatically employed every college graduate, male or female, who applies for a government job—provided he or she does not actually demand useful work. The policy was adopted because Egypt's commercial and industrial enterprises are too few to provide appropriate work for the flood of young, educated people with arts qualifications who pour out of the disproportionately numerous colleges and universities. Although in 1979 the statutory requirement to hire every graduate was lifted from some public companies, it still applies to many departments and, as a result, government offices are full of young officials who have nothing better to do than drink tea or coffee and make idle conversation with people waiting to see their superiors. The officials, in turn, employ an army of dependants who supply them with refreshments, run errands, carry messages or act as *bawabs* in the ministerial lobbies. And since the underlings are paid a pittance, they, too, are likely to demand a few piastres from a member of the public seeking access to a government official.

On the face of it, this system lacks any redeeming features. Yet it does have some virtue when seen in the light of traditional Egyptian values and the country's economic predicament. The senior officials, like the great

A shop in Cairo's Old City offers a variety of popularly priced imported footwear, including rows of the plastic sandals worn by innumerable Cairene women. Foreign shoes are gradually supplanting the unglamorous, but practical, sandals that are still made in Cairo from recycled plastic. In small workshops, waste plastic is ground to a coarse powder, heated and then pressed into moulds by pumps that often have been extemporized from the hydraulic brakes of superannuated motor vehicles.

landowners of the pre-revolutionary era, acquire prestige from the number of their underlings. The graduates find employment that otherwise would be unavailable. The coffee-makers, messengers and *bawabs*, like the graduates, gain sinecures without which the vast majority of them would be unemployed. The net result is that Cairo has relatively low unemployment figures, which benefits the government: people with jobs—even poorly paid and unproductive jobs—are less likely to challenge the political status quo than people who are out of work.

The attitude of the ordinary citizens to their administration is mixed. On the one hand, they will react energetically to demonstrate their criticism of the government in no uncertain way when an issue touches them closely. In October 1974, for example, some 2,000 citizens protesting at the inadequacy of public transport set fire to a bus station in Cairo and attempted to seize a rail depot; and in January 1977, the regime's stability was seriously threatened by massive riots that followed a sharp increase in food prices. On the other hand, they will often ignore official actions completely; for Cairenes have a healthy scepticism of authority in general —a legacy, perhaps, of centuries of foreign domination, during which they found the behaviour of their rulers incomprehensible, and largely irrelevant to their own lives.

The Cairenes' natural disregard for authority is expressed in many ways, not least in their anarchic driving habits. Few drivers take the precaution of using their rear-view mirror, and the few existing traffic signals are rarely obeyed even when policemen are nearby. Not surprisingly, Cairo's rate of traffic accidents—more than a thousand fatalities every year in a city with about 300,000 motor vehicles—is among the highest in the world, about 11 times higher than that of London and about 16 times that of New York.

A more positive aspect of the Cairenes' independent attitudes is their self-reliance in solving everyday living problems. A good example of how Cairo contends with the inadequacies of the official administration is provided by the system of garbage collection. The authorities have never developed a comprehensive municipal refuse-collection scheme, but provide only for the collection of garbage dumped at a few specified sites at street corners or on vacant lots. Judging by the piles of rubbish that permanently disfigure these spots, even that service is less than adequate. By contrast, however, door-to-door garbage collection is supremely well-organized by the private enterprise of two immigrant groups: the Wahiyah and the Zabalin. The former, a group of Muslims from the Dakhlah Oasis in the Western Desert, buy the rights of collection from the owners of rented property and make a service charge to the occupants of the buildings. The Zabalin, mainly Christians from the Coptic villages of Upper Egypt, buy the franchise from the Wahiyah middle men and undertake the actual collection. The charges to a building vary according to the income level of the occupants and the likely value of the garbage they throw out, since the Zabalin do not get paid for the work they do but make a small profit by scavenging items fit for re-use.

The Zabalin are one of the most despised segments of the populace, yet most of them have a cheerful air. There are some 40,000 of them, living in miserable shanty towns on the outskirts of the city. In Cairo itself, you can see teams of them at work almost any morning: two or three men, dressed like scarecrows in straw hats and an assortment of odd garments, and their children, making their rounds with a rickety, box-shaped donkey cart piled high with rubbish. Flies swarm around their cargo and their persons. Nonetheless, they seem to approach their work with a self-respecting stoicism: a boy may be singing as he drives along perched on his load of garbage; if you greet the drivers, they invariably smile back and wave a friendly hello; even their donkeys seem to trot with a business-like briskness.

When I first came to Cairo, I admired the good humour of the Zabalin and acknowledged that they were doing a useful job; but I did not realize that these humble workers were making an important contribution to the economic life of the capital until I happened to meet Dr. Sharif al-Hakim, one of Cairo's leading sociologists. Dr. al-Hakim had made a special study of the Zabalin. His explanation of their work was so interesting that I resolved to see a Zabalin shanty town for myself.

I drove out to the largest of their settlements by way of the dusty slums of Matariyah, built on the site of ancient Heliopolis, the Greek name for the long-vanished city where the ancient Egyptians once studied astronomy and worshipped the sun, and where the Greek philosopher Plato came to learn how the Egyptian astronomers calculated the exact length of the day. I drove down a street that was partly awash with sewage, and crossed a railway line where a dead donkey, covered in flies, lay beside the track. At last, after a tortuous drive around pot-holes, puddles and builders' excavations, I came to the edge of Cairo's urban sprawl and saw, beyond a field of ripening maize, the Zabalin settlement.

From afar, it looked like a typical shanty town: a jumble of ramshackle dwellings built of wooden boxes and flattened, rusty petrol cans. As I came closer, however, I saw that the shanty town was set amid a huge *maqlab*, or rubbish tip. Garbage was piled high in huge mounds around the shacks: rags, waste paper, rotting vegetation, tin cans, assorted metal objects and other refuse. The air was heavy with a queasy, over-ripe smell. Inside the doors of the makeshift dwellings I could see women and children picking over smaller piles of garbage and sorting the salvageable items into heaps.

Every month the Zabalin extract about 2,000 tons of waste paper, which is recycled into some 1,500 tons of paper and cardboard. They also provide cotton and woollen rags to be processed into upholstery and blankets; tin to be pressed and soldered into pots and pans, rivets, children's toys and

Reared by the Coptic Zabalin for sale to non-Muslims, pigs root for food on a garbage dump in north-east Cairo. The shanties are the homes of their owners.

Salvaging a Livelihood

In settlements built among refuse heaps on the city's outskirts live Cairo's 40,000 Zabalin —Coptic immigrants from Upper Egypt. In these insalubrious surroundings, which lack all civic amenities, the Zabalin make a living from pig breeding and from a highly efficient private enterprise system of garbage collection that also supplies recycled materials to the city's small factories and workshops. Each family helps collect rubbish daily from the city, sorts the re-usable items for sale and feeds the waste food to its pigs. Although their way of life exposes them to the constant risk of disease, many Zabalin families eventually accumulate enough savings to retire comfortably to their home villages.

Beside a mound of rags, a boy rests on the scale used for weighing salvage.

Cheerful Zabalin children take a moment off from helping their mothers sort garbage. The men and older boys are responsible for collecting Cairo's rubbish.

even spare parts for machinery; bones to be used for making glue, paints and a kind of high-grade carbon employed in sugar refining; glass and plastic for reprocessing. The sorting operation is so thorough that dry-cell batteries are even cracked open for the carbon rods inside, and the battery cases are melted into zinc ingots. All these materials, and many more, return to the economy of Cairo through bulk buyers and middle men who make substantial profits.

I left my car and walked along the main dirt track leading through the settlement. At the roadside were a few donkeys and sheep; nearby, a pack of yapping dogs were engaged in a Rabelaisian courtship. The flies were everywhere and, as I passed the shacks where the Zabalin kept pigs in crudely built wooden enclosures, there was the acrid stench of manure. The Coptic Zabalin are not affected by the Koranic ban on eating pork, but the fact that they rear the animals contributes to their low status in Cairo's predominantly Muslim society.

The pigs, I learnt, are a serious health hazard, since they attract vermin and disease-bearing flies, and so contribute to the exceptionally high mortality rate: four out of every 10 Zabalin infants die in their first year. The figure could be reduced significantly if the pigs were housed in a compound at a distance from the dwellings but, unfortunately, the Zabalin will not co-operate sufficiently with each other to take this step. Individual families guard their own livestock jealously since the animals represent their principal source of income. The variety of pigs that they breed for the meat and sausage market—supplying other Copts and non-Muslim visitors to Cairo—can produce two or three litters a year, and a litter may be as large as 20. A Zabalin family with 10 sows can earn about £E2,000 ($3,000)—a reasonable income in Cairo. In addition, the pigs contribute to the efficiency of the garbage recycling. The organic matter in the refuse is fed to the pigs; whatever the pigs do not eat, as well as their manure, is then turned into compost that is sold for agricultural purposes.

By Western standards, the living conditions I saw in the shanty town were appalling; yet the Zabalin have little incentive to improve them, since they can be evicted whenever the land they have occupied by squatting is required for further urban expansion—a process that has already com-pelled them to move again and again. But there can be no doubt about the value of their work in economic terms; the problem should perhaps be seen as one of improving their social conditions without sacrificing their activity. Although there are no figures available, the value of the salvage obtained by the Zabalin must run into millions of dollars annually. To import modern garbage-collection machines and techniques would be to throw 40,000 people out of work and to disrupt the hundreds of small factories and workshops that depend on recycled material for their products.

I asked Sharif al-Hakim for his opinion on the future of the Zabalin. "I think the social conditions could be improved with proper urban planning, without destroying the system. The Zabalin should be given the right to establish permanent settlements with housing of better quality. Their carts could be gradually mechanized, and workshops and factories placed near the settlements, to be near the raw materials. It would reduce transport costs and the exploitation of the Zabalin by middle men, giving a better return for their salvage."

Walking through many of Cairo's districts, I have been reminded time after time of the importance to the capital's economy of the ingenious recycling of which the Zabalin provide such a conspicuous example. Since labour is cheap and plentiful, and imported goods and raw materials are still relatively scarce and expensive, it is often more economical to re-use old materials than to create or purchase new ones; indeed, for many people it is virtually the only option available.

In dozens of second-hand clothes shops close to the Bab Zuwaylah, workers patch up or cut down cast-off garments that have become ragged and torn at the seams. In the side-streets off the Shari' al-Mu'izz, baskets of second-hand shoes are offered for sale, together with leather trimmings from the tanners with which to make repairs. Wood—a scarce commodity in Egypt—is utilized to the maximum. Sawdust and chippings are used as fuel by glass-makers and foundrymen. Old planks and boards are made into cheap furniture. Suitable fragments are used in making *mashrabiyah* screens for windows, sometimes on machine lathes but sometimes, too, on the traditional lathes that are turned by a bow and string. Indeed, the characteristically Cairene art form of the *mashrabiyah* was a direct consequence of the scarcity of wood; the interlocking pieces that make up the panels of lattice-work between the main frames can be made from small or twisted scraps, such as the smaller branches of fruit trees.

Most districts of Cairo have their share of small workshops using some kind of recycled material. Even in one of the cemeteries, near the tomb of Qa'it Bay, for example, I came across a factory where men were making domestic glassware from broken beer bottles, shattered mirrors and other discarded fragments of glass. There is an ironical side to glass manufacture in Egypt: since much of the country is covered by sand, an important raw material for glass, it might be assumed that there is a thriving, home-supplied industry. But, in fact, the sand of the Western Desert is of a type unsuitable for this purpose. In order to mass-produce glass, therefore, Egypt has to *import* sand. Such measures are beyond the capabilities of small-scale producers—hence the recycling industry.

The factory I found was nothing more than an ordinary mud-brick house —possibly once a tomb—with a blackened dome in one corner of the courtyard. The dome served as the chimney of a primitive furnace, around which three men were blowing glass bubbles through metal pipes and shaping them with tongs. Bare to the waist, their heads and shoulders

glistening with sweat, they worked with a frantic intensity, barely noticing
my presence. For me, the heat became unbearable after no more than
two or three minutes inside that inferno.

The bowls, tumblers and vases made in such workshops are to be found
all over Cairo. They are cheap and popular with tourists and foreigners.
Their colours, achieved by careful sorting of fragments, are similar to those
of old Venetian glass—blues, pale pinks, greens and browns—and their
irregular shapes and the air bubbles trapped inside give them charm and
lightness, making up in simple elegance for what they lack in sturdiness.
Also, if you break a piece of glassware in Cairo, there is consolation in the
thought that, when you throw it away, the bits in your dustbin will
eventually find their way back to a factory.

The heavy end of the recycling industry is located in southern Shubra,
an area of middle-class apartment blocks and small businesses that lies to
the north of Bulaq. Any open pieces of land are used as auto-wrecking
yards and metal foundries, and they are covered with the remains of
obsolete tractors, military vehicles, sections of buses and stacks of crankshafts, axles, steering columns and wheels.

I spoke to the young manager of a small business that specialized in
breaking up trucks for their spare parts. His father had started the enterprise 25 years before and he himself had worked there since the age of
seven. Trade, he explained, was still moderately good, in spite of a gradual
increase in the availability of foreign cars and parts as a result of the open-
door economic policy of 1974. He could pay up to £E3,000 for an old

Bedford truck and still make a small overall profit by selling off the parts, usually to other specialist dealers (in ball-bearings, crankshafts and the rest) but also direct to the general public. There were no quoted prices; every transaction was individually negotiated, according to the immemorial Egyptian custom. Nor were records kept of sales, since this would necessitate the employment of a bookkeeper—more than he could afford to pay out of his annual profit of about £E3,000. Not surprisingly, he had been in trouble with the taxman for the last seven years.

As we talked, a customer came in carrying an axle-bearing with a dented casing. The manager combed his yard for an exact replacement, but could not find one. Nevertheless, he sold the customer an axle-bearing similar to the one he had brought in. The customer, he explained later, was quite satisfied to get a part as near to the original as possible; he would then take it to a metalworker's shop to be filed down or otherwise adapted; there would be no problem in fitting the new part to the vehicle.

In every district of Cairo you can find small garages with mechanics (most of them boys in their early teens) performing feats of surgery on battle-scarred vehicles. Invariably, their workshops look chaotic: miscellaneous tools, wires, tubes, nuts and bolts lying higgledy-piggledy in the dust, dogs scratching themselves in corners, and perhaps a sheep searching for titbits among oily rags and newspapers. Yet, somehow the work gets done—and effectively, as is proved by the large number of ancient jalopies that can be seen in the streets of Cairo.

Mechanics' workshops are just part of a huge, city-wide network of small-scale private industrial workshops—about 150,000 in all. A small foundry might be found in a crumbling 17th-Century *wakalah*; a metalworker's shop may operate in a former café vacated by a Greek proprietor who had left in the 1950s; a carpentry business may be based in the garage of an apartment block. Then there are the many artisans who have set up small businesses in wooden shacks, in courtyards or in the street; in Cairo's almost rainless climate, the sky is cover enough for most activities.

Such is the proliferation of small businesses that it is difficult to walk down any street without encountering some such private enterprise. One day, for example, I explored a street in the run-down district of Bulaq. In one shop a blacksmith was welding hooks on to metal rods to make catches for doors; outside, on the sidewalk, a youth was using an oxy-acetylene torch to cut flanges from old steel piping; a few doors along, a welder was turning out metal bases for weighing scales; nearby, workers in a small foundry were casting the frames used for shaping domestic tiles and piling up the completed stock in the street.

Altogether, Cairo's small workshops and craft businesses employ about half a million people—an average of about three persons to each business. Even taking into account such constraining factors as lack of capital and

A herd of camels—painted with brands to indicate they are fit for slaughter—block an underpass in their languid progress to a state-controlled abattoir.

the shortage of materials and factory space, it would seem to make sound financial sense for some of these tiny individual enterprises to pool their resources and expand their businesses. But Cairenes do not determine their priorities solely on the basis of financial reward. The manager of the wrecker's yard explained to me over cups of black tea that he was not in the business simply for profit; equally important to him was the *barakah*: the intrinsically satisfying quality of the work itself.

The Muslim concept of *barakah* has no equivalent in English. The word, which derives from the same Arabic root as the verb *baraka*—"to bless"— has a religious connotation and conveys the notion that certain things in life, whether it be raising a family or doing a useful job, have a sacred quality, being, as it were, the wish of God. It might seem an odd concept to apply to work in a junkyard; nevertheless, it aptly expresses the attitude of many Cairenes towards their working environment.

For the self-employed Cairo citizen, there are other advantages. Since the majority of them live at or near their place of work, they are spared the stress of travelling on public transport. And they are not restricted, either socially or in business, by the shortcomings of all the communications systems the modern business world relies on. Theirs is a world of direct contact in a tightly knit community. They can meet to conduct business transactions in the local tea-house and return home for a meal in the middle of the working day. At the family level, theirs is a caring community, that provides work—or financial support—for relatives who are unable to find employment elsewhere because of age, sickness or other hindrance. Seen in this light, even the employment of young children sometimes can be justified. Officially, child labour is outlawed; primary schooling in Egypt, compulsory since 1922, has been more widely available since the post-revolutionary school-building programme. In reality, however, the law is so widely ignored that Cairo's private industry would collapse over-night if it were deprived at a stroke of its child workers. But most of the children work alongside close friends and relatives, and by learning a family trade they are arguably better equipped to survive in Cairo society than those students who gain academic diplomas and degrees that merely serve to qualify them for a lifetime of unproductive government employ-ment at $60 a month.

The alternatives to both these courses are to work abroad or seek em-ployment in a state-owned industry, such as the mammoth Halwan Iron and Steel Works 15 miles south of Cairo, which employs several thousand workers from the city. Built in the 1960s with Russian financial and tech-nical aid, the £E500 million ($750 million) project has been dogged by problems. The Soviet experts pulled out before completion and, although American engineers moved in to help complete the works and to graft computer mechanisms on to the existing plant, Halwan was running at less than half its annual 1.5-million-ton capacity in the late 1970s—a

In the courtyard of an ancient caravanserai within the densely populated Old City, where workshops and small industries compete for space, an upholsterer puts the finishing touches to a mock-Louis XV chair. Such heavily gilded French-style furniture first became popular among Cairo's aristocracy in the 19th Century and clumsy reproductions continue to be firm favourites among the Cairene bourgeoisie.

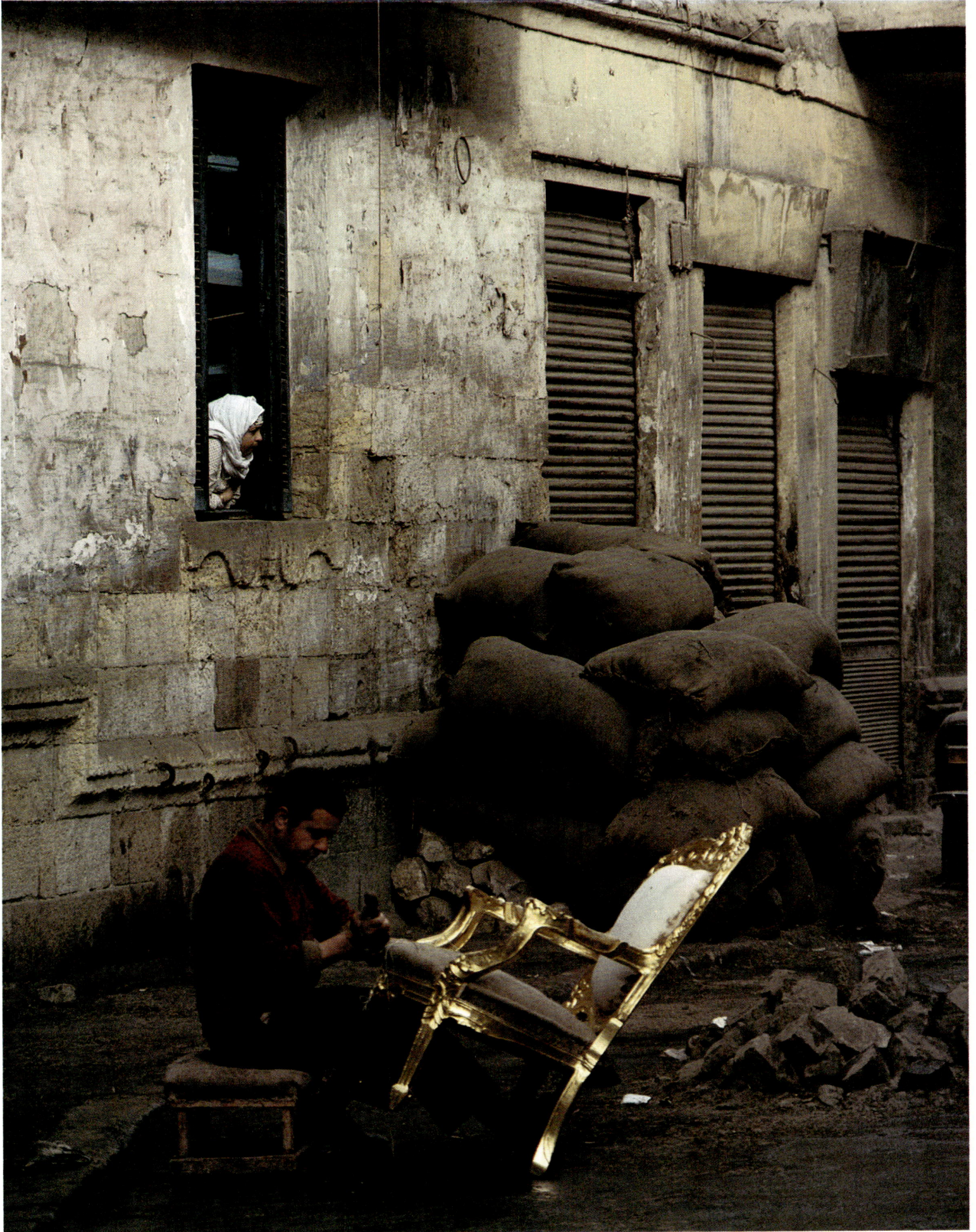

shortfall blamed on the inefficiency of the managers and bureaucrats rather than on any deficiencies of the plan or the work-force.

For an employee at the Halwan works, the advantages of assured employment and a living wage must be set against the problems of travelling to and from work. Most of the work-force live in the northern Cairo suburbs of Shubra and Shubra al-Khaymah, and have to commute to their work by bus to the tiny three-platform rail terminus at Bab al-Luq, where they catch a train to the Halwan complex. The journey is, quite simply, horrific. A shortage of passenger coaches means that the trains have to carry 200 per cent of their official capacity. Even more alarming is the regularity with which fatal rail crashes occur on the over-extended line, that serves 10 million passengers a year. And regularly, I hear shocking stories of boys who, in seeking a cooler ride, have hung on to the outside of carriages and been killed by trains travelling in the opposite direction.

The bus journey between the station itself and the workers' homes is scarcely less of a trial than the rail trip. I have never braved the journey myself, but I once took a bus all the way from the outskirts of Heliopolis to Tahrir Square—a distance of some 15 miles—and I feel I understand the problems they must contend with daily. My vehicle was one of Cairo's fleet of ancient and traffic-scarred buses, that seem to soldier on from year to year more or less unaffected by occasional injections of more modern buses into the system. There were only two other passengers on board when we set out from the terminus, and we rattled and swayed at a fair speed through the spacious boulevards of the modern suburb. But once we neared the centre of Heliopolis, the bus quickly filled to capacity with passengers who boarded not only at scheduled stops but also at every pause caused by crossroads or traffic jams. By the time we had covered half the distance, there were passengers perched on the mud-guards and clinging perilously to windows and doors.

Miraculously, a large and powerful woman managed to force her way on board while balancing a basket of fruit on her head. Someone elbowed her and a cascade of apples, pomegranates and figs tumbled into the throng and rolled around the dusty floor. A few kindly passengers tried to rescue some of the bruised and squashed fruit, then a quarrel developed over responsibility for the incident. The woman insisted it was not an accident and soon everyone on board joined in the altercation, gesticulating furiously in spite of the cramped space. In view of the heat, I was amazed that they had enough energy for an argument. When we arrived at Tahrir Square, an hour after setting off, I was exhausted and dripping with sweat—even though I had been one of the fortunate ones who had had a seat all through the journey.

Naturally enough, few Egyptians who can afford private means of transport will venture to board buses, streetcars or trains, but there are not marked advantages in owning a motor car. The traffic jams that plague

Off-peak travellers wait at the central bus terminal in Tahrir Square. Cairo's inexpensive but overburdened bus service carries three million passengers daily.

Cairo mean that, at peak travelling time, it can take an hour or more to drive a mere mile from the city centre. Many great cities, of course, are notorious for traffic jams, but none, in my view, can compete with the Cairene variety in terms of noise and smell. With its wild orchestration of hooting horns and revving engines, and its suffocating mixture of exhaust fumes and dust, a Cairo traffic jam is on a par with the visions of hell conjured up by Dante or Hieronymus Bosch. Boxed inside an automobile, you have the choice of two agonies: open the windows and choke on the dust and obnoxious smoke given off by cheap-grade petrol, or keep the windows closed and be slowly roasted as if in a pressure-cooker.

Another peril that motorists have to contend with is the large number of draught animals employed in Cairo. "Look at them, the bastards," cursed a furious taxi-driver as we swerved to avoid a donkey cart hauling a load of rubbish. "They ought to be cleared off the streets." An estimated 100,000 vehicles in the city are drawn by horses and donkeys, and they make a major contribution to traffic jams. In addition, it is not unusual to see flocks of sheep and goats on their way to or from a market, holding up traffic along the Corniche by the Nile, or in alleys near the slaughterhouse in the southern district of Sayyidah Zaynab. You could well imagine that the animals, vilified by motorists, are regarded as allies by pedestrians who see traffic snarl-ups as the means by which ambassadors in their limousines, business executives in their Mercedes and Peugeots, and gilded youths in their flashy sports cars are made to experience the kind of discomfort suffered by ordinary folk who have to rely on public transport.

Non-motorists in Cairo still fondly recall the spectacular camel stampede of 1977 as one of the great victories in their running battle with motorists. Normally, the camel is a phlegmatic creature that views the world with haughty disdain—a superior manner, so legend has it, stemming from its privileged knowledge of the hundredth name of God (the Koran divulges only 99 names to man). On this occasion, however, an entire herd of camels, roped in the traditional manner behind a herdsman on his donkey, and destined for the slaughterhouse, somehow became crazed and ran wild through the city streets.

I do not know what precipitated the stampede. Perhaps the scent of a female of the species in season had roused them, like the bugles at Balaclava, to a final charge of heroic folly; more probably they had caught the smell of death as they neared the city's main abattoir. Whatever the cause, they broke loose from their ropes and loped off in the opposite direction, towards the Nile. The result was magnificent confusion as cars, buses and trucks were forced to brake suddenly or swerve off the road to avoid the stampede. The camels blundered on, over a nearby bridge, on to Rawdah Island, across the island and over the Gama'at Bridge, until they reached the west bank, where they came to a halt and, oblivious of the chaos they had caused, began to graze quietly on the luscious tropical foliage near the zoo. There they were eventually rounded up and returned, by truck, to their place of execution.

The problems that Cairo's road-users have to contend with are an example of the conflict between traditional habits and modern needs—in this case between the slow pace of animal traffic and the demands of efficient motor transport. The same conflict reaches epic proportions in the fight to keep Cairo's population within the bounds imposed by available housing, jobs and services. So long as the capital continues to have the lion's share of services and employment opportunities, it will remain a magnet for the poor. The scale of the problem can be gauged by the fact that, while Cairo had about 25 per cent of the country's population at the end of the 1970s, it had two thirds of Egypt's television sets, half its telephones, one third of its doctors, two thirds of its college graduates; and it consumed almost 30 per cent of the country's power and about 40 per cent of its meat.

One solution is to divert people away from Cairo into outlying new towns that would also siphon off some of the government services and industries now concentrated in the capital. The first step in this direction was taken in the mid-1970s, when long-range plans were drawn up to establish three satellite cities in a ring about 30 miles from Cairo. Each new city is designed to have about 500,000 inhabitants and provide jobs for 185,000 by the end of the century. They will also be the first new cities to be built on unproductive desert land. But new cities will barely scratch the surface of Cairo's difficulties, if Egypt's population continues to grow at its present rate. Unless the birth rate falls drastically, by the year 2000 the country's population will have almost doubled to 70 million, of whom 20 million will be living in Cairo, which has an overall growth rate almost one third higher than that of any other Egyptian city.

Population planning is a sub-industry in Egypt, with literally hundreds of agencies involved. There is, however, a national plan. Drawn up by the Supreme Council for Population and Family Planning, it aims to halve the growth rate in the 1980s, mainly by changing people's attitudes towards the size of the family. Unfortunately, the plan is stricken with the same bureaucratic malaise that affects most official enterprises. Responsibility for its execution rests not only with the Supreme Council, but also with the ministries of Education, Religious Affairs, Information, Culture, Health, Social Affairs, Local Administration, Manpower, Land Reclamation and Agriculture, and the Arab Socialist Union.

Even if all these bureaucratic hurdles were surmounted, the people who have to put the plan into effect have the formidable task of persuading the public that having fewer children is desirable and necessary. The main problem is not overcoming religious laws: Islam forbids abortion and sterilization, but does not condemn contraception. But for most rural

This man, sitting casually on a sidewalk, smokes a shishah (water-pipe) that demonstrates the ingenuity of the Cairenes in making use of all available resources. His hubble-bubble has been created by fitting a standard tobacco bowl and stem into the top of a discarded aerosol can. Cooled by its passage through the water that partly fills the container, the smoke is drawn up through the bamboo tube that is inserted into the air space at the top of the can.

Egyptians, as for members of many traditional societies, a large family is an economic and social necessity; and this attitude remains with them when they move to Cairo. In fact, children not only provide man-power for the city's mini-industries, but they can contribute to the family income in other ways, such as selling trinkets to the tourists. Since state pensions are inadequate for all but a few, children also provide security in old age—and familial care of the aged is a responsibility that is still dutifully fulfilled. Yet nowadays, infant mortality—though high in Egypt, at more than 119 per thousand births—is falling fastest in Cairo, and improving medical care also results in longer life and better health among the old. Such developments lessen the practical value of a large family; but the attitudes of centuries have not yet been reshaped, and the birth-control campaign continues to make little progress.

Inevitably, I fear, the modern world will one day catch up with Cairo and transform its economic life. The craftsmen will be forced out of their workshops into the factories, abandoning individual skill and ingenuity for anonymous toil on a production line. The leisurely, person-to-person conduct of business will give way to rapid transactions by telephone; the civil service will be rationalized, throwing many people out of work; and the donkeys, horses and camels will be cleared off the streets to make room for yet more motor vehicles.

Such modernization will undoubtedly bring long-term material benefits to Cairo; but I believe that it would be a great shame if this new order were to be achieved at the expense of the city's most valuable resource—the humane, intimate quality of its social fabric. For, although Cairo is at present struggling to cope with a massive explosion of population, I sense that among its teeming streets human relationships remain more highly prized than they are within cities where a more streamlined—but more neurotic—lifestyle prevails. The warmth and good humour of the Cairenes are priceless assets that have served them well in the past; I feel sure that they will sustain them through whatever changes the future may bring.

Bibliography

Abu-Lughod, Janet L., *Cairo: 1001 Years of the City Victorious.* Princeton University Press, Princeton, New Jersey, 1971.
Aldridge, James, *Cairo.* Macmillan, London, 1970.
Berger, Morroe, *Islam in Egypt Today.* Cambridge University Press. London, 1970.
Bird, Michael, *Samuel Shepheard of Cairo.* Michael Joseph, London, 1957.
Casson, Lionel, and the Editors of Time-Life Books, *Ancient Egypt.* Time-Life International (Nederland) B.V., 1966.
Cecil, Lord Edward, *The Leisure of an Egyptian Official.* Hodder & Stoughton, London, 1931.
Cottrell, Leonard, *Egypt.* Nicholas Vane, London, 1966.
Cromer, Lord, *Modern Egypt (2 vols.).* The Macmillan Company, London, 1908.
Dawisha, A. I., *Egypt in the Arab World.* The Macmillan Press Ltd., London, 1976.
Edwards, I. E. S., *The Pyramids of Egypt.* Penguin Books Ltd.. Harmondsworth. Middlesex. 1961.
Egypt and How to See it. Ballantyne & Co., London, 1908-9.
Evans, Trefor, ed., *The Killearn Diaries.* Sidgwick & Jackson, London, 1972.
Fakhouri, Hani, *Kafr El-Elow.* Holt, Rinehart and Winston, Inc., New York and London, 1972.
Fedden, Robin, *Egypt.* John Murray, London, 1977.
Frankfort, Henri, *Ancient Egyptian Religion.* Harper & Row, London, 1962.
Gilsenan, Michael, *Saint and Sufi in Modern Egypt.* Oxford University Press. London. 1973.
Guide-Poche Univers, *Egypt.* Éditions Marcus, Paris, 1976.
Hart, Jerome, *A Levantine Log-book.* Longman. London. 1905.

Hureau, Jean, *Egypt Today.* Éditions j.a., Paris, 1977.
Johnstone, Sir Charles, *Mo and Other Originals.* Hamish Hamilton, London, 1971.
Jordan, Paul, *Egypt, the Black Land.* Phaidon, Oxford, 1976.
Kamil, Jill, *Ancient Egyptians: How They Live and Work.* David & Charles, Newton Abbot, 1976.
Kees, Hermann, *Ancient Egypt.* Faber & Faber, London, 1961.
Kessler, Christel, *The Carved Masonry Domes of Medieval Cairo.* The American University in Cairo Press, London, 1976.
Landes, David S., *Bankers and Pashas.* Heinemann, London, 1958.
Lane, Edward William, *Modern Egyptians.* East-West Publications, The Hague and London, 1978.
Lane-Poole, Stanley, *Cairo.* J. S. Virtue & Co., Ltd., London, 1892.
Lane-Poole, Stanley, *The Story of Cairo.* J. M. Dent & Sons, Ltd., London, 1902.
Mabro, Robert, *The Egyptian Economy 1952-1972.* Clarendon Press, London, 1974.
McLeave, Hugh, *The Last Pharaoh, The Ten Faces of Farouk.* Michael Joseph. London, 1969.
McPherson, J. W., *The Moulids of Egypt.* Printed by N.M. Press, Cairo, 1941.
Mahfouz, Naguib, *Midaq Alley.* Heinemann Educational, London, 1978.
Mahfouz, Naguib, *Miramar.* Heinemann Educational, London, 1978.
Manning, Olivia, *The Danger Tree.* Weidenfeld & Nicolson Ltd., London, 1977.
Mansfield, Peter, *Nasser.* Penguin Books Ltd., Harmondsworth, Middlesex, 1969.
Mansfield, Peter, *The British in Egypt.* Weidenfeld & Nicolson Ltd.. London. 1971.
Marlowe, John, *Cromer in Egypt.* Elek Books Ltd., London, 1970.

el Masri, Iris Habib, *The Story of the Copts.* The Middle East Council of Churches.
Nelson, Nina, *Shepheard's Hotel.* Barrie & Rockliff Ltd., London, 1960.
Nyrop, Richard F., *Area Handbook for Egypt.* U.S. Government Printing Office, Washington D.C., 1976.
Pudney, John, *The Thomas Cook Story.* Michael Joseph Ltd., London, 1953.
Richmond, J. C. B., *Egypt 1798-1952.* Methuen & Co., Ltd., London, 1977.
Russell, Dorothea, *Medieval Cairo.* Weidenfeld & Nicolson Ltd., London, 1962.
Showker, Kay, *Fodor's Egypt.* Hodder & Stoughton Ltd., London, 1979.
Sladen, Douglas, *Egypt and the English.* Hurst & Blackett Ltd., London, 1908.
Stewart, Desmond, *Young Egypt.* Allan Wingate, London, 1958.
Stewart, Desmond, *Cairo.* Phoenix House, London, 1965.
Stewart, Desmond, and the Editors of Time-Life Books, *Early Islam.* Time-Life International (Nederland) B.V., 1967.
Stewart, Desmond, *Cairo 5500 Years.* Thomas Y. Crowell Co., New York, 1968.
Stewart, Desmond, *Great Cairo.* Rupert Hart-Davis Ltd., London, 1969.
Thornton, Guy, *With the Anzacs in Cairo: a Tale of a Great Fight.* H. R. Allinson Ltd., London. 1918.
Vatikiotis, P. J., *The Modern History of Egypt.* Weidenfeld & Nicolson Ltd., London, 1969.
Wahba, Magdi, *Cultural Policy in Egypt.* Unesco, Paris, 1972.
Waterfield, Gordon, *Egypt.* Thames & Hudson, London, 1967.
Wiet, Gaston, *The Mosques of Cairo.* Librairie Hachette, Paris, 1966.
Wilson, John A., *The Burden of Egypt.* Macmillan, London, 1956.

Acknowledgements and Picture Credits

The editors wish to thank the following for their valuable assistance: Mohammed Sid-Ahmed, Cairo; Yousuf el Alfi, Cairo; Dr. Lewis Awad, Cairo; Dr. Sayid Aweis, Cairo; Dr. Zeki Badawi, London; Leila el Badri, Cairo; Cecilia Ballo Etcheverria, Cairo; Irene Beeson, Cairo; Paul Bergne, London; Zahir Bishay, London; Mark Bowden, London; Soeur Emmanuelle Cinquier, Cairo; Derek and Pamela Cooper, London: John Cottrell, London; Dr. Norman and Ruth Daniel. Cairo; Susie Dawson, London; William Donaldson, London; Hassan Fahmy, Cairo; Omar el Farouq, Cairo; Hasan Fateh, Cairo; Abdu Gobeir and Jean O'Hanlon Gobeir, Cairo: Dr. Sharif al Hakim, Cairo; Dr. Abdul Haleem, London; Angus Hall, London; Dr. Hassan Hanafi, Cairo; Nawal Hassan, Cairo; Mohamed Heikal, Cairo; Edward Hodgkin, London; Bambi Iskandar, Cairo; Fatma Khafaghi, Cairo; Hala el Kholy, Cairo; Jacqueline,

Lady Killearn, London; Alan Mackie, Cairo; Peter Mansfield, London; Dr. Michael Meinecke, Hamburg; A. R. Mills, London; Anthony Mockler, London; Beejay Moffatt, London; Cynthia Nelson, Cairo; Amy Whittier Newhall, Harvard University; Fawzia Norris, London; Susan de la Plain, London; Hermione, Countess of Ranfurly, London; Dr. John and Elizabeth Rodenbeck. Cairo; Michael Rogers, London; Adel and Madame Mahmoud Sabit, Cairo; Stephanie Sagelbiel, Cairo: Sandra Salmans. London; Denis and Elizabeth Schneiter, Cairo; Magda Stambouli, Cairo; Peter Stocks, London; Claude Thillaye, Cairo; Muhammed Wahby, London; Nayra Walker, Cairo; Bridget Westenra, London; David Wilson, London; Giles Wordsworth, London; Christopher Wren, Cairo; Wilton Wynne, Cairo.

Sources for pictures in this book are shown below.

Credits for the pictures from left to right are separated by commas; from top to bottom by dashes.

All photographs are by Robert Azzi, Woodfin Camp & Associates, New York except: Pages 14, 15—Map by Hunting Surveys Ltd., London (Silhouettes by Norman Bancroft-Hunt, Caterham Hill, Surrey). 38—Courtesy of The Smithsonian Institution, Freer Gallery of Art, Washington, D.C. 102—Photo Bibliothèque nationale, Paris. 105—Reproduced by permission from The Sir Benjamin Stone Collection, Birmingham Reference Library. 108—Sirot-Angel Collection, Paris. 110—Thomas Cook Group. 110 (inset)—British Library. 112, 113, 115—The Illustrated London News. 116—Fox Photos. 118, 119—Popperfoto. 120, 121—Associated Press. 141—Bruno Barbey from Magnum Photos.

Index

Numerals in italics indicate a photograph
or drawing of the subject mentioned.

Filmsetting by C. E. Dawkins (Typesetters) Ltd., London, SE1 1UN.
Printed and bound in Italy by Arnoldo Mondadori, Verona.